The Souls of
Our Children

The Souls of Our Children

Lessons of Love and Guidance

SAUNDRA CORTESE

HarperSanFrancisco

An Imprint of HarperCollins*Publishers*

HarperCollins Web Site: http://www.harpercollins.com

HarperCollins,® 📖 ,® and HarperSanFrancisco™ are trademarks of HarperCollins Publishers, Inc.

FIRST EDITION

Library of Congress Cataloging-in-Publication Data:

Cortese, Saundra
   The souls of our children : lessons of love and
   guidance / Saundra Cortese.—1st ed.
   ISBN 0–06–251392–3 (pbk.)
      1. Parents—Religious life. 2. Parenting—
   Religious aspects. 3. Cortese, Saundra. I. Title.
BL625.8.C67   1997
291.4'41—dc21   96–37300

97 98 99 00 01 ❖ RRDH 10 9 8 7 6 5 4 3 2 1

Contents

For Maximo David Cortese
and all the souls of our children

Acknowledgments

Thank you, Maximo, for choosing me as your gateway. I have embraced our journey together every step of the way and look forward to our continuing life together. I love you, son.

Thank you, Oprah Winfrey, for the time we spent together, giving me the loving push and support I needed to create this book.

Thank you, Michael, my husband, for being one of my greatest lessons of love in this life and for being my partner in bringing Maximo here so that our journeys can be fulfilled.

Thank you, Seth and Sara, for being my nephew and niece. Thank you, Sara, for loving me and teaching me that listening and loving are sometimes all we need. Thank you, Seth, for your gentlemanliness and the ever-so-unconditional love you've always given me. You, Sara, and Maximo have taught me a great deal about the souls of our children.

I also want to thank all the wonderful metaphysicians, spiritualists, and friends who have helped me get from pain to joy, creating balance and freedom in my soul.

Thanks to Geoff Bullens for helping me with the mechanics of translating reams of handwritten pages into a typed manuscript.

Thanks to Barbara Moulton for being a teacher and a friend—and for her unbelievable grace and sensitivity in keeping me on track. Thank you, Lisa Bach, for your excellent editorial suggestions and for seeing the book through its final paces.

And for my spiritual brother—who is not only an extraordinary writer himself but is also a sensitive, compassionate, and funny man, and who helped me with the final editing of this inspirational book—Guy Kettelhack: thank you, my dear man. Working with you is more than a joy.

Saundra Cortese

Before You Read This Book . . .

One of the greatest adventures I have ever embarked upon is one I never thought I'd take: motherhood. For years I never thought of having children. In fact, I'd been actively warned against having a child. My mother, remembering her own devastating postpartum depression after I was born, told me, "You're very much like me, so I think you should be careful." A deeply intuitive woman, my mother was afraid of her own inner power. Having children deluged her with feelings she felt totally unable to handle. Her response was to shut down. She knew I shared this intuitive power, this sensitivity, but she couldn't imagine it being anything but negative. A beautiful woman physically, she tried to lose herself in appearances and shunned anything that required paying attention to anyone else. She also suffered from acute agoraphobia—a fear of open spaces, roads, stores, and travel—as well as an inability to tolerate being alone. The world was a frightening place to my mother, and having children forced her into more of the world than she felt equipped to deal with. She couldn't see her own inner power as a gift; she experienced it only as a burden. And she was sure I would react in the same way.

My mother's warning about having children gave me a powerful message. It didn't matter that whenever I saw a child my heart leapt lovingly. It didn't matter that when my sister had children I treated them with as much love and joy as if they were my own. When the prospect of *my* being a mother arose, I buried it; I was convinced my mother was right. Motherhood was not for me; I was not cut out for it. I was afraid it would smother the rest of my life. I was afraid I would feel, as my mother had, that a child was far more burden than gift.

So I poured my energies into a career. I became highly successful in a very competitive field, working in the garment district of Manhattan, traveling the world, making a good deal of money. Giving up that career for motherhood wasn't in my vision not only because of my mother's warning but also because of my observations of so many other parents, most of whom seemed locked in a power struggle with their children, attempting to "mold" them, change them, dominate them. What I had experienced of parenting as a child, and seen in the world around me as a woman, had never sat well with me—this concept of controlling another person's will and soul. I had fought hard against my own parents' dictatorial behavior: I didn't want to become a dictator myself. I knew that this parental control ultimately stole away individuality; the soul, coerced and controlled, became bound. I didn't want to fall again into that trap, the trap I had worked so hard to get out of—a trap that, as a parent, I wasn't sure I would know how to evade. I didn't want to become my own mother.

Then, in my late thirties—an age when many mothers have raised their children and are starting a career in the business world—I chose to become pregnant. Why this change of heart?

There were many reasons. I had, for some time, been exploring my own spirituality, and I had worked with a number of spiritual teachers. I once consulted a psychic from Barcelona, a man named Santiago, who told me he saw my child come into the world with a loaf of bread under his arm—a sign that the child was blessed. That thought never left my heart or mind. I also consulted Sharon Klingler, a metaphysician—that title coming from the Greek for "beyond the physical," which her gift of insight certainly was and is. An expert interpreter of Tarot cards, she told me in numerous readings about the energy of a little soul trying to come through me, asserting that this child was fine, healthy, happy—and very ready to be here. Then a dear friend of mine, Jacqueline, who for years had been unable to conceive, finally had a child—followed in quick succession by two more. "I'd give anything for you to have kids," she told me. The light in her eyes convinced me that she'd had a life-changing experience. One of the most helpful persons in my life for my change of heart was another one of my dearest friends, Marilyn. She chose to become pregnant even though she wasn't married to or permanently involved with the man who fathered her child. Her pregnancy was beautiful, and she was and is a beautiful mother—a powerful, positive example of a single parent. As new mothers, Jacqueline and Marilyn provided wonderful support and helped me to cross over the line with all their love. Today our children are best friends, as are we. Marilyn's daughter Zoë was actually born in the same month on the same day as Maximo, my son, although a year apart—which I know is more than coincidence. It was as if Marilyn had beckoned me to become the gateway to a child—a soul—that her own daughter ached to meet, play with, and grow with in this world.

I met Michael, my husband, first as a friend. Ironically, he was Marilyn's exboyfriend, and all three of us got along wonderfully well. I hadn't at first any clue that Michael and I would end up marrying; our relationship only gradually became romantic. However, slowly, with increasing strength, we realized that we wanted our paths to join, not only as friends but as partners in life. Our growing warmth and security, along with many painful lessons about intimacy, about learning to grow as individuals in the context of joining our lives as a couple, set the stage for our ability to conceive and give birth to Maximo.

But Maximo didn't come without a struggle. As if still bound by my mother's negative message, my first attempts to become pregnant ended in miscarriage. As I meditated and grew deeper in my spirituality, I began to realize that the soul of my son was trying again and again to reach me, come through me, be born into the world. I now know he couldn't come until I was completely ready for him—spiritually as well as physically. Michael also had to work through his fears of becoming a parent. His own childhood had been a troubled one, and he was afraid of the responsibility of bringing up his own child. My miscarriages seemed to indicate that we still weren't quite ready to receive the gift of a child.

Maximo was patient. The final miscarriage before his soul manifested devastated Michael and me worse than ever before—and made us realize not only that we truly *did* want a child but that we were finally ready to have a child. When I became pregnant again, under a doctor's orders I spent most of the pregnancy in bed, terrified that I might lose the precious opportunity to meet this soul who seemed to want so urgently to join me and Michael. Finally some spiritual receptivity fell into place: Maximo managed to be born. It was a difficult birth physically; the attending doctor badly mismanaged the delivery, necessitating a long and difficult recovery. It was as if Maximo and I had to overcome every obstacle in the world to give him life. But just as I overcame my mother's negativity by learning that I could positively channel the power inside me, I overcame—with Maximo's and Michael's help—the pain of giving birth. Ultimately, it all made his arrival even more of a joy and triumph: we had both gone through hell to reach the heaven of finally meeting here, in this world.

This realization that a *pact* had been made among Maximo, Michael, and me was one of my strongest spiritual lessons: getting ready for Maximo taught me, beyond any doubt, that the soul of my growing baby had sought me out. He wanted me to be his mother; he wanted Michael to be his father. In some way, I knew we had made an agreement to join paths; we had *chosen* each other. I also got the clear message, which intensified throughout my pregnancy, that I was participating in a miracle that not only would bring the child Michael and I yearned for but would teach me something to pass on to others. I began to evolve a new view of motherhood, of parenting—one very different from what my mother had passed on to me. It was as if the soul coming through me were telling me that parenthood doesn't have to be a burden. On the contrary, it's a magnificent gift. It doesn't have to be about control. It instead can be, and needs to be, a mutually caring bond—one in which parent and child teach each other in this lifetime, one that allows each of them to grow as their own souls wish them to grow.

I've said that I knew certain things spiritually about Maximo—that Michael, Maximo, and I had made a pact on the soul level, that we had chosen each other to be spiritual partners. How did I know this?

It's difficult to put the answer in words. The source of my spiritual certainty is as unknowable as God. However, as I've learned to trust my spiritual intuition, I've found that relying on it never fails. My sense of spiritual "knowing" wasn't, and isn't, limited to Maximo or the lessons of parenthood; I have always had a strong spiritual sense of everyone and everything in my life. Spirituality is something I've learned to develop, but it isn't something I willed into being. Initially it seemed to seek *me* out. I was aware, from early childhood, that my outer world masked an inner one, an eternal world of wonder, peace, and solace that underlay all the turmoil of the physical world.

A soul in his body form doesn't choose the circumstances of lessons to learn through but the individual does choose how to handle them.

Our conscious minds, our higher self is far greater than we can comprehend and we aren't going to always know the reason of every lesson, but if we can live in the moment and trust ourselves, create every lesson as an opportunity no matter how difficult, we will be able to support our higher selves with decisions and activity that help us attend to its lessons even if we don't always know the reason.

My first memory of making contact with this under-lying spirituality takes me back to age three. I remember standing up in my crib and looking into a mirror. It was as if I were recognizing myself for the first time, recog-nizing—becoming familiar with—the form my soul took in the world. I saw my face, my hands, and my body, and I realized something amazing: I *existed* as an individual. In those moments of discovery, I also realized that I had a *purpose* for existing. I had something to do, a mission to accomplish, a journey to take. At the time I didn't know what that purpose was. Through the years, though, it's become apparent. I am here to take my journey as freely as possible. Life offers me a road of great adventure, even if it's often paved with the stones of difficulty and pain. However, as young as three, I real-ized that I had not only the desire but also the will to follow wherever this adventure took me. I trusted that there was something spiritual at the heart of me that I could always rely on—and that would comfort, save, and guide me.

The greatest joy came from realizing I could follow this adventure *myself*. Because I wasn't embraced by my parents, it was hard to feel secure or have faith in or about myself. This awakening—at three—taught me that I could trust something deeper—something *within* me—to direct me. Slowly, as I felt this trust deepen, I knew more strongly that we're here to take our journeys freely, according to the dictates of our own hearts and souls—not according to someone else's scheme of things. It was a lesson that saved my life. My father was as critical and negative as my mother—as ill-equipped as she was to nurture a child. I realized very early on that there was no water in my family well. My older sister, angry that she no longer received the attention she'd gotten when she was the only child in the family, and affected by our mother's despair after my birth, rejected me from the moment I entered the world.

All of this prodded me to find water elsewhere. I found it first in myself. And the more I drank from that well, the stronger my trust became—and the stronger my resolve to live according to my own heart. Not that there haven't been scars: I still feel the reflex sometimes to limit my or Michael's or Maximo's journeys out of old, reflexive fears; my parents' negative criticism still echoes sometimes in my head. But I know now, as I first knew at three, that there's a far greater source of strength and wisdom than my parents' limited assumptions. I have learned quietly to reconnect with that source and get back on the right free-flowing track.

I believe each of us has access to that source. I also believe it's urgent that we develop the ability to access our spiritual selves, particularly if we choose to parent another soul. The children we bring into this world need spiritual nurturing in addition to physical nurturing. They must not be brought into this life and abandoned, physically and emotionally. Children who never enjoy unconditional love and acceptance are greatly harmed. We must learn to support and feed all children's souls from the very beginning. We must understand their individuality and respect them as equals. We must also realize that we're no greater or more important than they are. And *they* deserve to learn all this too, so that they don't turn into angry, lost souls. The task, as I've said, is urgent. I strongly believe that people who steal, rape, murder—or simply find themselves floundering from one unsatisfying relationship to another, from job to job, feeling no sense of purpose—never knew unconditional love and acceptance as children. Spiritual parenting isn't some New Age luxury; it's an essential skill every parent needs to develop. We all need to understand what it means.

As you read this book, I ask you to listen without making instant judgments. I ask you to look beyond your old assumptions, to resist jumping to conclusions. I ask you to set aside any belief that tells you there's only one right or wrong way to be a parent. In other words, I ask you to read with a truly open mind. Our children are the future, and our only hope for humanity. We need to learn how to let them grow into healthy and happy people, to be true to their souls, to follow their individual paths. As you read this book, you may see more clearly the negative patterns of parenting in our society—and perhaps in your own assumptions as well. You too can learn how to become a free soul—and how to help your children to become free souls. It's never too late. Your child's birth can be your own rebirth. Of course, rebirth can happen at any stage of life: the lessons and suggestions in this book should help to awaken you to your own soul strength, whatever stage of life or parenting you face.

The journey you and I will take begins with an exploration of what it means to be a mother, and then what it means to be a father. The chapter on mothers will concentrate mostly on the period of pregnancy, the period in which mother and child are most deeply bound—and that offers so many unexplored opportunities for partnership and communion between the souls of child and mother. While we'll also talk about the father's role during pregnancy, the chapter on fathers will push more into the territory of childhood, the period in which fathers usually play their largest role.

The aim is to help you not only to identify old and unhelpful assumptions about "mother" and "father" that may limit you but also to create new, more productive, open-ended assumptions that will lead you and your child to spiritual freedom.

Chapter 3 will discuss the arrival of a child, focusing especially on how to create a zone of protection and optimal stimulation for this new human being. Here, as elsewhere in the book, I will offer practical suggestions, from my own experience and the experience of other parents, to help you to create the most nurturing "soul environment" you can. Every suggestion in this book—even though grounded in day-to-day reality—is geared toward helping you and your child to cultivate your spiritual strength and create environments and circumstances that allow spirituality to flow within you. So much of what nurtures the spirit amounts to getting out of its way—letting the force inside you tell *you* who it is and what it wants to be, not the other way around.

This focus will similarly direct us throughout the rest of the book: dealing with siblings, embracing opportunities for communication, seeking the "grace" of discipline, dealing with the challenge of single-parenting, learning the value and delight to be found in play, and exploring the importance of *partnership* in this whole parent-and-child experience and in life's adventure. Ending with partnership rounds out our journey: just as we begin our lives as parents in a spiritual partnership, entering into a pact that I believe begins far earlier than actual physical birth, we end with an exploration of what partnership means in the here-and-now, on this earth—examining partnerships between father and mother, between parent and child, and in the many interactions each member of the family creates for him- or herself.

Ending on this note of partnership is one of the strongest parts of my mission: to show you that you're not alone in your journey as a parent. There's infinitely abundant and accessible love from which to draw, both from your own inner being and from the spiritual depths of others. Attending to this crucial aspect of partnership won't just improve the quality of your family life; it will do something far more important as well. It will help you to avoid some of the worst wounds all too often unconsciously inflicted on children who are brought into the world by fearful parents—parents who don't realize what Maximo and Michael and my own inner spiritual guidance have taught me: life is about joy and freedom, not anger and fear. This movement toward positivity, toward spirituality, will do more than improve your relationship with your children, partner, and family.

It will create a much larger vibration in your own world, and ultimately in the world beyond you. As you make your interactions with your family freer, more positive, and more joyful, that joy will spread to others. Attending to our own private spirituality has an inescapable spillover to the world around us. It's never been more urgent to set this positive chain reaction in motion.

For me parenting is a full-time job. I enjoy what I know is the luxury of being able to stay home and bring up my son; I gave up my business for the career of raising my child. I felt strongly that I couldn't devote myself to two careers and be successful at both. I realize, of course, that many women and men don't have that freedom of choice. Financial considerations force sacrifices in both areas. If you're one of those people forced to sacrifice, I understand and empathize with your struggle. I hope this book will be a map that will help you to balance all the pulls in your life. You must find your own path, but that portion of it devoted to parenting can be made much more rewarding. Fathers especially deserve empathy and consideration: the fact that culturally we still generally expect fathers to spend most of their daylight hours away at "work" doesn't mean we shouldn't mourn the fact that fathers often, through time constraints, can't be as present as they would like to be—or need to be.

However, whatever circumstances you face through choice or necessity, you can bring a more spiritual awareness to what challenges you—and often turn it to your advantage. This book will give you some hard-learned suggestions about how to do exactly that. We all experience the wellsprings of soul in different ways; each of us has a different definition of *spirituality*. But we all have access to this essential realm, and this book should help you and your children to increase contact with that realm within you—however you define or perceive it.

For all men and women who are, or want to become, parents, I want to share what I've learned about how to open the gates to the soul. The rewards are considerable: as more and more of us connect with our soul strength, we discover not only the best route to the tranquillity of living in harmony with our families but also how to bring harmony to the world.

Let's work together so that through our children the twenty-first century will be an age of peace and enlightenment.

ONE

So the Journey Begins:

ဆ *Mothers*

A free soul does not need to hurry. It does not know time as we do. It knows no schedules or deadlines, and so it waits—years, decades, even centuries—before it chooses one man and one woman to conceive a body for its new earthly journey. In that body it will remain for a lifetime, learning, experiencing, and teaching as it takes its journey.

In this chapter we'll focus on the mother—especially on the concept of mother as gateway for the soul.

I'll show you how to combat negative energy around you as your arriving soul grows within you, as well as introduce the truth that you can communicate openly and completely even while your growing baby is still in your womb.

Let's start with the meaning of *gateway*. Why am I so sure that concept describes the essential spiritual role of every mother?

As I've mentioned, I knew, as early as three years old (when I stood up in my crib and looked at myself in the mirror), something beyond question: that I was here on a mission—and that my life was a gift to enable me to carry out that mission. I understood that although my parents didn't often express love or concern for me, they had nonetheless given me the greatest gift imaginable: they had given me life. The concept of *gateway* came to me very early on. I soon understood that for some reason I had chosen my mother to act as gateway for my soul: as unhappy as she was, as unhappy as she so often made me feel, she still had something to teach me that I needed to learn—even if at first I wasn't at all sure what that "something" was.

As an adult, I was privileged to meet spiritual teachers on this plane who helped me to pursue the answer to that and many other questions, as well as open me to my own spiritual guides within: especially Santiago and Sharon Klingler, whom I've mentioned, along with psychic Maya Perez and many wonderful others. Helped by their insights, I gained a sense of the spiritual pacts we make with our parents—to be born, to learn various spiritual lessons from one another, along with so much else about the soul; that gave me a calmer and more clarifying understanding of life.

The function of mother as gateway became especially clear. Our mothers are the actual physical presences in whom we grow and from whose flesh we separate ourselves when we're born. We must literally pass through them to enter physical life. But mothers are potentially so much more than just the physical gateways for the souls that pass into this world. As mothers, we need to recognize that we've been chosen by another soul to be its gateway into physical life— and that we, in turn, have also chosen to bring this particular child, this soul, into this world. We also need to see that *every moment* we spend in the child's presence once he or she has begun, physically, to exist—starting in the womb—provides us with opportunities to be gateways for many of the baby's thousands of new experiences. By providing calm when we sense the little soul needs calm, by feeding ourselves appropriately, and by otherwise taking physical and emotional care of ourselves, we help, gently, to nudge and guide the souls within us as comfortably as possible through each stage of their development; we help them, as much as we can, to perceive the world outside as a welcoming place.

We are the gateway from the start. The day arrives when you stare at the results of a home pregnancy test, with the color blue or pink (or a plus sign) indicating "positive"—or maybe a call from the doctor's office. You say, "I did it! *We* did it! I'm pregnant!" You probably feel euphoric—and then, several minutes later, another reality may hit: "Oh, my God!" You put your hands on your stomach, and you feel scared. I remember this moment; indeed, because I'd had several miscarriages before I gave birth, I experienced the moment more than once. (I'm convinced the soul who eventually became my son, Maximo, simply refused to give up: when, physically and spiritually, I wasn't quite ready to accommodate him, he just came back and tried again!) I know these feelings of anxiety. The fear of the physical pain of birth. The overwhelming sense of responsibility that comes from realizing you have a *human being* growing in you, and that his or her well-being is up to you—*totally*.

But the fear can be instructive. It can help to put the next nine months into perspective. The realization of the tremendous responsibility you must now take on can help you to "put your house in order"—internally (emotionally) as well as externally. If you have fears, they often tell you what you need to do to prepare your nest. If it seems a monumental task at first, come back to living in the moment. Even the most monumental task gets done in a series of very small, simple, and achievable steps. Just concentrate on *now:* this will help you to decide on the steps you can take in the present. Don't worry about steps to come.

Seizing each moment to deal openly with every new encounter of motherhood is one of the great keys needed to unlock and release the healthiest attitude. Your unborn child grows and changes every second, and you can help your child by becoming as conscious of the present moment as you can, living through your growing infant's changes *with* him or her. The nine months your child spends inside the womb may seem slow to you as a whole block of time, but realize that the being you're creating is evolving at an astonishing rate that will never be equaled again in its lifetime, and that the experience of growth is a momentary one—measured in seconds, minutes, hours, days. Realize that every moment counts, that each moment is an important adventure. Become conscious of *now*—and you'll be more conscious of the miracle of growth your baby is undergoing.

While your baby evolves and grows in your womb, you'll begin to feel the soul around and within you. This can be an odd sensation. Sometimes the soul resides in the womb; sometimes it flits out and hovers near you. It never leaves, but you may perceive it as changing its presence. Only as the infant nears the end of its period of physical gestation does the soul return and remain mostly in the body.

As I've already said, I was aware of Maximo's presence from the moment of conception: it was every bit as strong then as it is now, as he stands in front of me, a growing five-year-old boy. Open yourself to the experience, accept the feeling, and the soul will become present to you. You'll feel its warmth and great energy. I communicated to Maximo's soul the day he was conceived: "I hope you took, child. I want you to be here." Allow yourself this moment of feeling your motherhood. Doing this can actually provide one of the surest routes of communication with your *own* soul, not just the soul of your baby; it connects you with a deeper, stronger flow inside. It helps you to create the soul environment in which you can hear and trust your own intuition. Communicating with your infant from conception on is one of the greatest ways I know of helping you to open the door to this whole vital realm inside you.

Advice regarding pregnancy traditionally deals with nourishing the body, not the soul. You're advised on good nutrition and physical self-care by a bewildering number of experts, in books, magazines, videos, and classes as well as by whatever prenatal caregivers (obstetricians, nutritionists, and so on) you may consult one-on-one. But these experts tell you only part of what you need to know. Sure, good nutrition and taking care of yourself physically help to develop a physically healthy baby, but this kind of care nurtures only part of the child's growth. Information on the emotional and spiritual health of tiny infants is scarce. Doctors rarely advise you on this; it's not part of their training. While the science and technology of aiding the pregnant woman have progressed astonishingly in the past century, the philosophy of spiritual development has received virtually no attention at all. The vast majority of expectant mothers understand little about what they're actually creating and carrying inside their wombs. If those tiny beings aren't spiritually nourished, they often come into this world already lost and angry.

In ancient times (and today in what might be referred to as more primitive cultures), the spirituality of the pregnant mother and the infant she carried received a great deal more attention. Many Native American tribes, for example, picked which man would couple with which woman based in part on the spiritual being they would together bring into the world. Grandparents in numerous cultures were regarded as essential sources of spiritual and worldly wisdom; their roles were far more crucial in raising children than they are in most cultures today. While these older cultures may have lacked our sophisticated scientific understanding and technological innovations, they were far more able than our own culture has been to create spiritually satisfied mothers, fathers, and children.

The pendulum has swung too far in the direction of science: it needs to be brought back into balance. We know that the child absorbs everything the mother absorbs physically: her nutrition has a direct impact on the fetus growing in her womb. But we don't realize that the mother's emotional and spiritual state has every bit as powerful an impact on her child. While this spiritual component can't be isolated or studied by science (the way, say, glucose can be studied in the blood), it's every bit as important. Luckily, nature generally breaches the gap. Intuitively, most mothers realize, on some level at least, that they share their spiritual thoughts and feelings with the infants in their wombs. But because science generally dismisses spirituality as so much fluff, we've never acknowledged how important this communion between mother and child really is.

The fear that acknowledging the spirituality of pregnancy and parenthood might sound crazy or embarrassingly "out there" is terribly misguided. This spiritual connection needs to be understood and explored, not dismissed or laughed at. Mothers must nourish their own souls so that their children can be allowed freely to nourish theirs. There exists no anatomical bridge for this, for it isn't biological or physical. The baby simply shares the energy of the mother's soul. We ignore this at our own—and our children's—risk. So many souls are born angry because they didn't receive the nurturing they needed from the start. They're the products of negative energy, which they absorb, like toxic substances, from the mother and father. Throughout pregnancy, it remains tremendously important that the energy coming from the mother is positive. Luckily, as I hope to make clear in this book, negative energy *can* be rechanneled into positive energy. In fact, as I learned early in childhood, you can channel that energy positively any time you want to.

You may be reading this book before you've gotten pregnant, during pregnancy, near the end of your term, or even long after your child was born. If your child is now five or eight years old, does this mean that this book has come to you too late? Has your child already been irreparably harmed by past negative energy?

No. Wounds can be the source of great wisdom. You can learn from pain as well as pleasure; indeed, pain often leads us to our most powerful revelations. Perhaps you became a parent at a very young age, which on its own may have caused problems: you may simply not have been mature enough or ready to be a parent. Perhaps you grew up with the idea that a parent's main job was to enforce strict rules, to "keep a child in line." Your child may, as a result, be painfully shy or the victim of terrible rages. You may only now realize the damage that was done, however unwittingly. But you can learn to call on different reserves now and redirect your journey. It's never too late. You can replace anger and fear—even when they're deeply entrenched—with love and spiritual peace. You and your children may have to work through some painful growth, but you *can* learn to live from love, not fear. Wounds may leave scars—but they can heal.

I know this because of my own wounds. I certainly know the effects of negative energy. As I said, my mother was, for her own painful and blocked reasons, incapable of giving me much nurturing. She was an intuitive, sharp, physically beautiful woman—but she was stuck in her body. My father tended to live more for his own mother's needs, always trying to make her happiest. This caused him, unfortuately, to loose sight of his partnership with his wife. As a result, there was a black hole where spiritual acceptance and unconditional love ought to have been: both my parents were absent in this way. Somehow, though, I was lucky enough to understand very early on that this negative energy wasn't good for me. More than that, it wasn't the truth. It was a distortion of the truth: the flow that *wanted* to happen in me was full of joy and freedom, not rage and terror.

So I began to seek sources of positive energy elsewhere in my life. Two were especially lifesaving. One of them was my grandmother—a woman who was disliked by many in my family. She'd had a difficult life, and she behaved bitterly toward a lot of my relatives and my friends, but she never was bitter with me, the youngest. I never saw the negative in her; I saw only the positive. I know now that that's why she responded to me so lovingly. She gave me the model for motherly behavior—making the lunches, making sure the projects were done—that I follow with Maximo. Her wisdom helped me when it felt as if all the other family members had turned their backs on me.

My other great spiritual source was my dog. I was given a dog who lived for seventeen years and taught me everything I know about unconditional love. Receiving unconditional love teaches a person how to give it. I loved my dog as much as she loved me. She helped to save my life. But the experience of love received from my dog and my grandmother taught me another more general lesson: it taught me that I had the power of gentleness and patience, and it revealed the difference between good and bad environments. With the help of love, I learned that I didn't have to stay stuck where I was. It taught me that I could—and in my childhood I *had* to—find for myself what I couldn't get from my own guardians, my parents. Some of this resource, as I've said, was internal; some of it was external. The experience of love also helped me to believe that there were more loving presences in the world with whom I could connect. Maybe life could be as wonderful outside as sometimes I could make it inside! The love I felt from and for my grandmother and my dog affects me just as strongly today: whenever I see unattended animals or older people who are alone, my heart is drawn to them, and I take whatever time is necessary to see that they're okay. This creates a chain reaction: I've passed this sense of caring and unconditional love on to Maximo, who shares it with the people and animals in his own life. Positive history repeats itself: in fact, you can't stop this love from spilling over to other people—it's contagious.

However, because there's still so much fear and suspicion in the world—creating negative history, which also repeats itself—those outside positive sources aren't always easy to find. I've learned that true positive energy is as rare as it is powerful. It takes great strength and effort to free yourself from the shackles of negativity. I know, because I've managed to do this over many years in my own life (and I still wage the battle). But you must break the chains that bind you, for they'll also bind your child. It may mean finding love in a pet, or cultivating a new friend, or getting in touch with someone you once deeply cared about to resume a needed positive relationship. *It's important.* When our "charge" is negative, it's conducted instantly to our children; in fact, I believe it affects them from conception on. Therefore, from the moment you know you're pregnant, make a concerted effort to be positive about your pregnancy.

I know this is sometimes easier said than done. "Negative" emotions such as sadness, anger, depression, and confusion—perhaps at the news of our pregnancy, throughout our term, and/or after the birth of our child—afflict all of us to different degrees. They can be difficult to dislodge because they're so often connected unconsciously to old family baggage—fears and superstitions we all inevitably drag into our lives. I had one recurring, disturbing dream during the early part of my pregnancy. I dreamed of pushing my child in a wheelchair in the supermarket. In my waking life, I was terribly anxious that Maximo be born healthy—with all his limbs in working order—and obviously my dream was built on that anxiety. Because I was an older mother (as I said, I became pregnant at the age of thirty-nine), I knew that statistics said I was at greater risk for giving birth to a disabled child. But unless I addressed that concern, I would communicate my anxiety to the child growing in me.

Sometimes, however, the little soul within fights back. One day I got a clear message from my own growing little soul: "Cut it out!" his spirit told me. "I'm fine!" After that, every time the old anxiety reemerged, the sense of Maximo's spirit would pipe up at me again to cut it out. He was comforting *me*—assuring me that so many of my worries were unfounded.

There are other worries you may share. The reality that in the nine months of pregnancy you'll grow large and uncomfortable. The fear of change—not to mention the fear of being unattractive. You need to change your vision of yourself. Life in the process of renewing itself can never be ugly. Your body will return to form—possibly a bit different, and maybe even better. The reward—acting as gateway for a new soul to enter this world—far outweighs these necessary pains and changes. Do something wonderful for yourself and your new spirit: gaze into the mirror every day and see the beauty of the miracle. Inside you, a life is growing, and you're blessed with the power to bring it into the world. Don't resent the process—or at those moments when you do resent it, remind yourself that you're participating in the renewal of life. Remember that discomfort, fear, and confusion are normal blips on the screen. Return to the moment. Imagine yourself as the baby inside, innocent and growing, and rejoice in the miracle.

In order to prevent or counteract any feelings of rejection and to ensure the health of your baby's spirit, communicate as fully and positively as you can with the child from day one. Of course, science tells us that the brain doesn't develop until a certain time, but the spirit isn't housed in the brain, or in any other physical organ. Talk to your child's soul; connect with it. As soon as you begin to communicate, you begin to respect your child's individuality. Sometimes the energy he or she sends can really surprise you. Before I became pregnant,

I loved tuna and ate it often. But when I was pregnant with Maximo, I could barely eat it. I'd often heard that mothers' food preferences changed during pregnancy, but those changes were always blamed on hormonal fluctuations. However, sure enough, after Maximo arrived and had his first taste of tuna, he made it clear that he could definitely live without it. He does, however, love bagels—which I can attest to by the number I suddenly had the craving to eat (every day) when I was pregnant!

Let the baby inside you feel your excitement and happiness, not only by telling those around you about it but by putting your hands on your stomach and sharing your feelings with the creation inside you. Tell your child's soul, "I love you." Say that you're willing to undertake the responsibility of caring for him or her. If you concentrate and focus on the moment, receive the energy of that little soul's love, you'll get back a response: "I love you too."

Protecting the soul from negative energy often involves changing habits, making sacrifices. Unfortunately, it may even mean, in some cases, losing friends and others close to you. This can be painful and make you feel very alone. Some of my friends weren't supportive of my decision to become a mother at thirty-nine; after a while, when I found that they couldn't change their attitude, I had to look elsewhere for friendship and support. Not surprisingly, some of my family members completely ignored the whole process of my pregnancy and giving birth. This hurt but didn't surprise me: they had long ago proven their inability to give anything of themselves to others. As I mentioned earlier, the doctor overseeing Maximo's delivery damaged me internally during the birth. He didn't take the usual "exit care" required in the treatment of mothers my age and thus caused serious tissue-tearing; nor did he sew me up properly afterward. I continued to experience severe pain because of this for a long time after Maximo's birth. Dealing with the pain, along with my raging hormones, made me concerned about falling into postpartum depression. My friends told me about an herb called sepia, which helped me enormously. It helped to regulate my hormones, and as a result I never suffered from the postpartum depression my mother had predicted—not a moment of it. Spiritually, I helped myself immeasurably by allowing myself to live in the moment, simply by looking at and experiencing the miracle of little Maximo. "Oh, my God, what a gift!" I said, again and again. I'm convinced this helped to heal me not only physically but emotionally—and it taught me the most important lesson I've learned: live in the moment. See the baby in your arms; don't obsess over the past or the future; live now.

If any experience teaches you to "live now," it's having—and bringing up—a baby. And living in the present teaches you how important a positive environment is—and how ruthless you sometimes have to be in ridding your environment of people and circumstances that aren't nurturing. If you surround yourself with a crowd of angry or indifferent souls, you and your child will absorb their negative energy like a sponge from the sea. Trust your intuition. Surround yourself with the healthiest, most positive souls you can find, and you'll feel the difference both when you're pregnant and when your newborn is in your arms. This positive influence can sometimes be brought about in unanticipated ways. Three houses away from my summer home lives a neighbor I used to wave at from time to time during the summertime but with whom I otherwise had no contact at all. When she found out I was pregnant, she made herself available as a friend, lovingly organizing a baby shower for me and sharing her own experiences as a mother. Sometimes just the knowledge that you're facing motherhood can open up new capacities in people. Allow this to happen. Don't resist the entry of new, positive people. They can come from surprising places.

They may turn into some of the best friends you and your baby will ever have.

If you find yourself in a physically unhealthy environment and you can't simply leave, take control of the scene and create a healthier environment on your own. If smokers are near, ask them please to extinguish their cigarettes. Tell them why, and if they take offense, remove yourself. You don't want to be with the negative energy of their selfishness. Avoid noisy and chaotic places: they'll breed confusion in the soul you're carrying. Keep safely out of reach of people who are cynical, bitter, angry, or depressed, even if they're close to you— even if they're members of your family. Remember, hurt feelings can be mended, but your child's soul will carry its wounds into life. It's defenseless in the womb, and you're its only shield. Protecting that soul 100 percent of the time is difficult because you'll always encounter unavoidable noises, smells, and other unpleasant circumstances over which you have little control. But if you work to give the baby in your womb a majority of positive experiences, whatever wounds those negative influences cause will be minimal.

Inevitably, you'll encounter those mothers who delight in recounting in great detail how horrible their labor was. These are women's versions of war stories:

triumphing over incredible pain and anguish. Look for the humor in these stories (there's almost always a good deal of it!), and remember that no two births are the same. Worrying about labor pains months before you're due clouds your spirit and produces negative energy. Once again: live in the moment and don't fear the experience. Nature will take over when the time comes, and the birth will be beautiful. I'm not overlooking the difficulties: I've told you about the physical misery I faced when I gave birth to Maximo. But despite that misery, the act and fact of birth remained beautiful to me. Our very existence proves that the pain will not be unbearable. Keep your thoughts and purpose clear, and focus on the present. Whatever happens, you'll bear it, and it will very probably not be the nightmare you sometimes fear. One thing I was often told: no woman would give birth to more than one child if giving birth were unbearable!

You may also meet women who say that they got pregnant and zipped through the nine months hardly thinking about it. This, to my mind, isn't something to brag about. This is neither loving, nurturing, nor fair to their unborn. If you go through pregnancy with this attitude, then you'll most likely go through life unconscious of your child's feelings. If you're feeling oblivious to the burgeoning life within you, catch yourself. Start now to seek and recognize your child's soul. Realize that the very energy of your attitude can make or break a situation; and this situation, the development of your child, is too important (to both of you) for you to ignore or discount.

You must reach out to the soul of your child. Forge the bond that will in turn bring you more in touch with yourself. Then you'll see and feel the wondrous beauty of pregnancy, the miracle of creation. This will create clarity of mind and body for you, your unborn child, and those around you. Hope that the father of your child will take your lead. As actively as Michael grappled with his own ambivalence about being a father before I was pregnant with Maximo, once I was pregnant, Michael bloomed. He became the most caring, the most sensitive helpmate I could have wished anyone to be. He discovered in himself new capacities for love and responsibility. Remember: though you're the gateway, you and your partner are both responsible for the finished product. Beckon to the father of your child to take part—and joy—in the miracle both of you have made possible.

Achieving this clarity of purpose means being considerate of your unborn child's growth process and individuality. In fact, *consideration* is a key word for you, and for your partner, for the rest of your lives. Consider every day, week, and month that your child is growing. Read about the process, the physical stages of fetal development. Bookstores are full of clear, illustrated guides, and your own prenatal caregiver has probably provided you with a good deal of explicit literature on the subject. Know and understand in which particular week the precious little hands and feet will grow, or in which particular month the lungs are developing. Understand and be clear on what you can do to help the development. Please don't make the mistake of thinking that your unborn child will develop perfectly well with or without your help. The physical fetus may grow on schedule without your intervention as long as the care is adequate, but the soul within can flourish only if you love it—and behave as if you love it. Praise your baby during pregnancy as you plan to after he or she is born. Tell your child how beautiful his or her hands are or how powerful the heart will be. Let your baby know what a great job he or she is doing, creating him- or herself.

I wrote many journals during my pregnancy, sharing my feelings and thoughts with Maximo. Investing in a notebook might be a good idea for you too. But you needn't limit sharing your feelings to your notebook, or to silent communication with your unborn child. Turn to friends—particularly friends who have children or are expecting children themselves—and share your insights. Pregnant mothers have far more to tell each other than health or diet or exercise tips, or who gives the best obstetrical care. They have much to share about feeling, and dealing with, the mystery of creation going on inside them.

You can share even your negative feelings. Indeed, you can't *help* "sharing" them with the being in your womb: that soul feels everything you feel. Learn to acknowledge every emotion openly. Any feeling or thought I had during my pregnancy I shared with the soul in my womb. I thanked that soul for his part in allowing me to come to whatever new insights I had managed to achieve. I knew it was pointless to try to hide anything from this growing being. Everything I felt, thought, and experienced during these nine months, my baby also felt, thought, and experienced. It came through my body and from my soul. Even sounds in the room—the sounds of my and his father's voices, the television, the radio, a car honking in the street, the patter of rain on the roof— happened as completely to Maximo as they did to me or Michael. He was also absorbing my emotions—my happiness and my sadness. Maximo and I communicated, worked out—even sometimes laughed together over— every moment of our shared lives.

I truly felt that Maximo communicated back to me. One thing he made clear: he preferred rock-and-roll to Vivaldi. Even though I enjoyed Vivaldi, when I played it during my pregnancy I felt uneasy. I couldn't reach the notes when I tried to hum along with it; it just didn't sound or feel right. But when I played anything with a rock-and-roll beat, that rightness returned. I felt a calmness—almost an enjoyment—from Maximo. As with tuna and bagels, after he was born and could communicate physically, he confirmed these likes and dislikes: even before he could speak, he'd squirm at Vivaldi and coo at the Beatles. (At the age of four he learned all the words to another rock-and-roll beat, "Give me a ticket for an airplane. . . .") And I explained what I felt needed to be explained when Maximo might not have understood on his own. Sometimes this meant just being honest about my passing anxiety and sadness. I'd let him know what my feeling was, explaining that it didn't have to threaten him. He didn't have to be afraid whenever things didn't go well; it wasn't the end of the world. Sometimes you had to go through bad feelings to get to good ones.

Give of yourself, and you'll receive. This means that if you put forth true effort in communicating your feelings, your visions, and your love to your unborn child, and if you travel through the pregnancy with a clear mind and spirit and with the genuine understanding of why you're pregnant, you'll respect the body and soul that you carry. In turn, the soul you're bringing to earth will be born clear in mind and spirit.

During your pregnancy, another transformation takes place: yours. You leave girlhood behind and cross through the gates into womanhood and then motherhood. You're traveling nature's incredible and beautiful cycle. You were born, and soon you'll give birth. As the months progress and your body grows with your child's, your mind moves deeper into motherhood—an area that so many of us question. Will I be a good mother? How will I do this? Will I act properly in difficult situations? This is the time to use your will, your power of intuition. Your will is your strength to do what feels correct. Trust your intuition; it's your guide. Only *you* know the answers to your questions—not your friends or your mother or your grandmother. Be aware that not everything that's been handed down to you through generations of mothers is correct. Listen to and absorb advice, but let your intuition guide you in your choices. History has repeated itself for centuries, and as the years have gone by, certain misinformation has been magnified, the lies coming to seem more powerful, as if they were truth. For centuries, but perhaps most damagingly in the Victorian era—to whose strict rules of childrearing we're still reacting—children weren't regarded as "children" at all. They were treated as, and expected to behave and work like, little adults. This dismissal of childhood has given rise throughout the decades to such misguided notions as "Children should be seen and not heard"—and to the general notion that children are somehow less important than adults.

It's now time to break those entrenched belief patterns. They're outdated, and the present state of the world stands as a testament to the fact that they don't produce healthy souls. It's been said that we come into this world as originals and leave as copies. It's time to change and transcend that: to remain originals throughout our lives. The concepts of *mother* and *child* must take on new meaning. *Child* isn't less powerful or important than *mother* or *father:* all are equal souls, all are equally deserving human beings. In the chapters to come, you'll learn not only how to cultivate your and your child's spirituality; you'll also learn how we all can turn the tide of history and make a better future by bringing into this world clear, healthy, individual souls.

TWO

*In Gentleness
Lies True Strength:*

ɤ *Fathers*

A soul chooses its mother and father to conceive its
body, but it also chooses them as its teachers and
guardians. While the mother's journey involves the
physical growing of the baby, the father's position in the
circle of life is no less extraordinary. The journey of fatherhood involves giving pure love, showing compassion, and teaching each soul the couple brings onto this
earth that he or she is an individual and the parents'
equal.

ɤ 43

As a father, you need to give great mental and emotional support to both mother and child. But the best way to begin to take on the responsibility of your journey as a father is to be open with and close to the mother. She's the carrier and gateway for the physical child you've helped to create. As a father, you need to assume a new position. A man's life changes course when he and his partner conceive a child, and it can never change back. Michael—my husband and Maximo's father—had as hard a time coming to this idea of parenthood as I had, and for some similar reasons. He too had received little comfort or love in his own upbringing; his father was as absent in his life as mine was. But he now feels as strongly as I do that Maximo came to change both of our fearful and negative blocks against parenthood. When we conceived, Michael was as joyful as I was—and he recognized how important his role was right from the start. Maximo heard his father's voice constantly: he knew both of us were planning for and expecting him with joy.

There will certainly be some obstacles ahead in the path to fatherhood—some of them coming from old, damaging assumptions about fatherhood that you learned from your own ancestral paternal chain—but it's a path, once begun, that must be traveled, and it's ultimately one of the most wonderful experiences in life.

Taking this journey and living up to this ultimate responsibility stands as the test of a true man. When a woman becomes pregnant, the man is like a gardener who has planted his seed. Now he must nurture his flowers with gentleness and love. This process begins not after the plant has grown and bloomed but at the moment the seed takes root. The father must nourish that seed—the unborn soul—and keep it healthy. If he doesn't, he increases the likelihood that his seed will grow into a bitter crop—with a tendency to be dysfunctional and unbalanced. Human "seeds" that aren't nourished properly are unaware that they're receiving less love, less caring, less compassion than they need. From birth they search for what's missing—the positive energy that would fill their souls and bring them peace. The lack of care they've suffered is hard to replace: their wounds and their hunger for love often run deep. Their peace and well-being have been shaken by the positive words not said, by the love not given to them from the beginning.

As I've said, though, wounds can heal. You can do much after the child is born to repair the damage you may have done by not offering enough spiritual sustenance during pregnancy. The child him- or herself may also discover—as Michael and I fortunately did—a source of spiritual solace and strength within. But how much happier our passages would have been if our parents had known how to feed us spiritually, from conception on! If you have the opportunity now, during the vital period before birth, to send out love and positive energy to your growing infant, do everything in your power to keep that love and energy flowing.

The hard truth is that not everyone is as fortunate as Michael and I have been in finding the inner resources to heal from the pain of spiritual malnutrition. We all know people who were undernourished in this way, raised by uncaring gardeners. They often carry dark legacies of fathers who weren't nurturing or loving to the bodies and souls they helped to produce. Like the flower, the body will grow without love, but it will never achieve maximal beauty. Never reaching its full potential, it may wither and die—symbolically at first, physically later. When a garden is nourished properly, flowers grow tall and glowing. Though they're strong, they can bend with the breeze and thus never break. They're sturdy in root, healthy in form, and beautiful in appearance because their gardeners took responsibility for loving and caring for them.

If a man plants his seed and it takes root, a new child's body begins to form, and a soul steps into that body. The father now must take responsibility for it whether or not the pregnancy was planned by the father and mother. A higher power has chosen them for an even higher purpose. Now the man must take on his fatherly role, just as the woman becomes a mother. A positive fatherly role means accepting that you're out of the nest: that *you* now have to build a nest for others and provide for the souls in your care. It means not only taking responsibility for your child and the mother of your child but taking responsibility for yourself. Your actions now have real consequences. Sometimes, of course, you'll resist. Becoming a father is potentially as terrifying as becoming a mother. Issues deriving from our painful childhoods continued to crop up for Michael and me even after Maximo's birth. For example, when Michael was playing with Maximo one day, he was struck by a deep sadness—thinking how incredible it was that his own father had never found the time to play with him when he was a little boy. But that sadness eventually cleared the way to joy, as Michael realized what a gift he's capable of giving to his own son. In some spiritual way, getting down on all fours with Maximo and zooming toy cars and trucks across the living room rug helped make up for the play Michael never experienced with his own father. He was not only providing Maximo with spiritual nurturing; he was nurturing himself.

The idea that a man and woman could live in harmony with their children was strange to both Michael and me, because neither of us experienced harmony between our parents when we were children. (My parents divorced when I was still a little girl; and Michael's, though they stayed together, barely communicated whenever his father was around.) We knew, as we faced Maximo's arrival, that a lot of marriages break up after the arrival of children; we didn't want to follow that same path. What Michael and I both learned in addressing that concern is that we needed to face the pain, recognize it—for the moment, not fight it. Even when our fears or disagreements were greatest, we learned to be honest about our feelings. We also learned to set clear boundaries. It was unfair for either of us to abuse the other because of issues we were going through privately. We learned a truer and deeper consideration for each other: the same respect for each other we brought to Maximo. These weren't lessons we learned overnight: they came only through much pain and great turmoil, out of which slowly developed patience and the ability to communicate with each other.

There are some wonderful fathers in this world who serve as models. They know their task as the gardeners of life and their importance as the guardians of life.

When you look around and see a father being gentle and spending time with his children, speaking with great respect to them, playing games, participating in sports, reading, eating meals with them, putting them to bed, playing kissy-face (the most wonderful game in the world!), laughing—then you're seeing a great father. Unfortunately, there aren't enough of them. The new father must realize that whatever he did and whoever he was before is now part of history, because his journey in life has changed. He must accept this within himself. I think of this process as "learning to go home"—home to your truest self, a home different from the ones your own father and grandfather (and so on) may have built for themselves. You undoubtedly have dreams for your child, fantasies of the person you'd like him or her to be, but learn to listen to the dreams your child has and help him or her to achieve them. As with the mother, negative associations and anyone or anything not supportive of your new journey must be left in the past. If this can't be done alone, seek the help of positive people to keep you living in the moment.

When the word *mother* is spoken, we make certain associations, have certain feelings or visions. When the word *father* is spoken, it sometimes invokes other, opposing visions, too many of them angry, competitive, or cold—visions that history has unfortunately reinforced (the personal history of many of us as well as the history of men in the world). Slowly the image of the father as forbidding disciplinarian is changing, however; decades of feminism and Steve Martin movies have helped to deflate some of those old assumptions. And many men are naturally affectionate and caring and nurturing, of course. But as I look around at parents in the world, it amazes me how common the old stereotype of the Big Bad Daddy still is.

As a father, you can choose to balance old ideas of fatherhood with more loving role models. Raising a child in spiritually nurturing ways requires that balance. Picture the yin-yang, the Oriental symbol that depicts the balance of life. While the child grows inside the mother, it must connect not only with her but with the father as well. The father can talk to and commune with his unborn child just as easily as the mother can. One friend of mine says he owes his love of music to the fact that his father, who had a beautiful voice, always sang to him—even when he was in the womb. And Michael talked to Maximo—both in the womb and as a newborn infant—about finances! "I'm going to teach you how to keep your finances in order," he'd say with mock formality to his infant son, a twinkle in his voice. "You're going to understand the pure and simple facts of keeping track of your money." Today, at five, Maximo is already clearly a "numbers man": he's fascinated by numbers and arithmetic. Who knows whether he learned some of this from Michael before he was even born? Michael loves to joke and laugh—which Maximo does too, partly from having heard his daddy joke and laugh from the moment he was conceived.

Your baby will miss nothing, so communicate to him or her in the most positive way you can. Let your child hear your loving voice. Fathers need to express their happiness to their children—born or unborn—and put forth their positive energy. They need to put equal effort into communicating with and understanding the mother: a growing infant in the womb feels the love between father and mother and starts to learn about communication and compassion. Fathers need to realize that when the mother is near, so is the child near, soaking up energy like a sponge. That's why fathers need to stay clear-minded about their purpose and intentions. We never know what the infant absorbs from our conversations before and after birth. You can try to communicate anything you want—even advice about finances!—as long as you keep your tone loving.

Interestingly, the one break a father receives during the pregnancy is the ability to remove himself from the new soul. Because he isn't carrying the child, he can detach himself physically from both mother and child in ways the mother obviously can't. This private time is a good opportunity for the father to begin to restructure his life, to understand the new direction of his journey. This private time is good for the mother as well. A father needs to understand that it isn't necessary for him to be around the mother every moment, that she needs private moments to increase her own special bond with her baby. A father can also use this time away to diffuse any negative energy that he might be carrying. This might mean losing himself in a pleasurable hobby, making plans for the baby's room, or reorganizing financial priorities in anticipation of the new arrival. When he returns to the mother and his baby, he needs to clear his mind of negativity and return with love. There's never an excuse for not showing love to mother or child. This must be the father's first priority.

This is never more true than in the common case of a father coming home from work—perhaps angry or grumpy from an exasperating day. The basic structure of our society demands that we work; it's a given. And as we all know, it's in the workplace that much negative energy is acquired—but unfortunately not released. Pent-up anger, stress, and frustration from the job often release themselves at home. This scenario is all too common, and of course it's not limited to fathers. Many pregnant mothers work throughout most of the term of their pregnancy and have to deal with the same workplace frustrations as do men. Problems come when reprimanded or stressed-out workers fail to communicate their feelings in the moment; holding those feelings in, workers internalize the negative energy, which festers and grows until they get home to what seems like a "safe" place to lash out. In fact, lashing out without thinking of the consequences is never "safe"; it always wounds. Indeed, it's the ultimate sin that parents commit. The home is no haven for anger—and how unfair to put a child (born or unborn) in such a trapped position!

As I've said, this dilemma is by no means limited to fathers. But because mothers are generally far more aware that they're carrying a child than fathers are, they often understand more readily the need to maintain a calm and loving attitude. Fathers—especially before the child has been born—are more apt, for the moment, to forget their parental role. They may tend to take out their anger on whomever they find when they come home—which can have harmful consequences. In fact, misdirected anger lies at the root of many problems our children have. Through the eyes of a child, consider the example that's been set: Dad walks out the door, disappears for hours to a place called "work," and returns distracted and tense. Sometimes he returns yelling; sometimes he just walks into his study and shuts the door—without even a hello.

Coming home from work is one of the most crucial times for fathers to remember that they *are* fathers—to think about how their actions will affect their children, whether before or after birth. When the father of a growing soul goes off to do what he has to do in life, he must remember not to return with negative feelings left over from an unresolved confrontation. Spreading such feelings to loved ones is neither respectful of them nor loving to them. Learn to deal with conflict in the moment; communicate your frustration and anger to the right person—the person with whom you're actually in conflict. If further conflict remains, or if the problem seems irresolvable, remove yourself from the situation and reevaluate your motives, your circumstances, and what you want the outcome to be. No job or negative situation is worth sacrificing the soul and healthy growth of your child. If you return from work full of negativity, try explaining to your spouse and child, "I had a really bad day; I'm not sure of my feelings," or "I need some time alone before I can talk"; alternatively, explain the source of your frustration and ask, "What do you think of this situation?" If you're simply too angry to manage those kinds of reasonable responses, take a silent moment to ask yourself, "Am I really angry with my family, or is it still my boss, who dumped all that extra work on me?" Go ahead and tell your family you had a bad day, but make it clear that your negativity has nothing to do with them and assure them that after you take some time to chill out you'll be able to be more positive and loving. These open and honest attempts to diffuse anger work, breaking the negative-energy domino effect. The mother of your children, as well as your children (before or after birth), will return this gift of respect and love to you. Keep your journey clear in your mind, let the positive energy flow through and around you, and do what you can to force the negative energy out.

It's not that you won't sometimes "fight"—every family experiences and expresses conflict. But fight in the moment: talk about what's really bothering you; don't take out on other people (or expect them to cure) what in fact doesn't concern them. Allow yourself your emotion, allow your partner her emotion, allow your child his or her emotion—but learn to stay in the moment. The unborn child who experiences this conflict will also experience its resolution—and learn that it's possible to get through these inevitable rough spots.

One way to ensure the abundance of positive energy is for fathers to surround themselves as much as possible with positive people, at work, at home, and at play. A new father who keeps going back to watching Monday Night Football with his old bachelor buddies may find that he isn't accepted quite so easily any longer; he may feel that these "free" men don't think they have much in common with him anymore. If you're in that situation, you may be a little hurt, but you need to break that old connection. If you can't forge a new connection to your friends based on a free, full acceptance of who each of them is, it's time to move on. You have a choice: you don't, in most cases, have to stay around people who affect you negatively, who fill you with anger or frustration. Some closed-minded people might not like you once you cross through the gates into fatherhood. Don't let yourself be brought down by them. Everything moves and changes, nothing stays the same, and none of us is an exception to this universal law. To resist the pull of the universe benefits no one. If you continue to surround yourself with unaccepting people, you'll be in a continual state of conflict.

Fathers need to understand that every action they take has a direct effect on their children. Parents often tend to focus too much on what *they* think the child needs rather than listening to the child and observing his or her needs. Yet nothing we do for our children needs to be done with such intensity; we need not obsess over our actions or theirs. As a father, you shouldn't say, for example, "I want my son to get the most our of life." Instead, help your child to explore his or her own interests. The necessary balance is achieved through love, respect, communication, and patience. Each child is gifted in his or her own way. Trying to think *for* your children doesn't help them. Let them think for themselves, and be there to guide and protect them. Don't seek to make them your mirror image. Let them follow their paths as individuals. Don't punish them for not being like you, because your journey is yours and theirs is theirs. Once again: find the love in your expectations.

Sometimes fathers treat their friends better than their children. Respect for individuality and attention to needs, thoughts, and feelings comes naturally with friends—and not so easily with children. If you place a child on a level lower than you, the result is that you invalidate him or her. *A child is no less important, no less an individual, than an adult is.* Every child deserves to be validated—completely.

If a man can't understand how to take his journey of fatherhood, it may be time for him to review his position as a son to his own father. Remember the time that Michael felt sad when he was playing with Maximo? In that moment of sadness, he was actually reviewing his own relationship with his father, recalling once again the lack of love and attention he'd received. But that little moment of "review" became, ultimately, an occasion for joy: Michael can feel good now that he's grown enough to be able to give Maximo something his father couldn't give him. As a new father, you automatically remember yourself as a child with your father. Don't concentrate on the unhappy associations that come to mind, however; if you get mired in what wasn't good in your past, rather than what was good, you're in danger of passing your negative feelings on to your child. Give yourself permission to enjoy the happy memories as well. Michael always thinks of his father at Easter, for example, since it was his father who put together his Easter basket annually. It must have made them both feel very good, because every Easter of Maximo's life Michael has created Maximo's Easter basket—and the baskets have been getting bigger and bigger every year. Think about the times your father made you feel good about yourself. Reflect on some of the specific things your father said or did that made you feel good. Whatever these positive messages or activities were, be grateful for them. They've planted such goodness in you that you'll automatically want to pass them on to your own children.

Of course, not all your father's messages were so positive. Replaying the bad times—and then letting them go—is as instructive as replaying the good. Any feelings of invalidation your father may have planted in you can help you to be on the lookout for similar problems as you deal with your own child (problems that, without the thoughtful scrutiny that results from the consideration of your own history, might remain unconscious). History repeats itself when we refuse to analyze old invalidating patterns. We need to replace those patterns with new and better ones. Think of the sayings that invalidated you in the past. If you aren't careful, you may find yourself uttering to your children those same echoes of the past.

The following selfish, invalidating, disrespectful approaches to communicating with children will probably sound familiar to you:

- "Children should be seen and not heard" is the motto of selfish, ignorant parents who lack the ability to see children as individual minds and souls. This mentality has adversely affected more than one generation, holding back masses from communicating extraordinary thoughts. Try instead to affirm your love for your child by saying, "I'm so glad that you're my son [or daughter]. I love being around you. You're lots of fun to be with."

- "No, because I said so" and "No, because I'm your father [or mother]" deny a child the experience of learning why. Children weaned on these sayings often grow up with a dangerous curiosity, because they haven't been taught the why of what's risky or safe. Alternatively, they may grow up with absolutely no desire to question the universe—numb, deadened. Try, instead, a response such as this: "No, because now isn't the right time. Maybe we can do it another time. Thank you for understanding." Always thank your child for respecting you. The word *no*, when said with sharp emotion, should be reserved for danger. It's a vastly powerful word that must be used wisely. In situations involving safety, let your child know that you're afraid he or she could get hurt. Never say, "You'll get hurt!" unless injury is a strong possibility.

- "Don't speak unless you have something intelligent to say" is spoken by invalidating parents who were invalidated themselves and pass this tragically inhibiting thought on like a hereditary disease. Instead, try, "Tell me what you think. Your opinion is always important to me." Then make sure you listen.

It remains essential that we, as fathers and mothers, step back and monitor ourselves and our behavior. We often circle back subconsciously to some of the negative parenting habits of our own fathers and mothers. Try to see yourself through your child's eyes. Are you scolding or punishing your child because it's necessary, or because you were irrationally scolded or punished for a similar act when you were a child? Even parents who swore they would never do what their parents did or say what their parents said find themselves doing so. When we're under stress (and therefore unable to review a situation calmly and objectively and select a course of action), we simply replay the scene from our own childhood—only now we're the parent. You must fight against this by destroying these "tapes" when you come upon them, reprogramming yourself to react in a rational manner. And don't forget to pay attention to the *positive* habits of your parents too: remember the messages that *validated* you. Emulate those positive traits, and be glad you experienced them in your own parents. You can make your own child feel as good as those messages made you feel when you were a child.

One of the traps that men often fall into as fathers is the use of intimidation in the effort to control. Threatened by my free spirit, my mother would often get angry and make me go to my room, warning me that my father would punish me when he got home. Never once questioning my mother's decision, my father would come home, storm into my room, and strap me with his belt (or simply grit his teeth and growl at me, which scared me to death). We never bonded. As a child, I was so afraid of my father that I couldn't even look him in the face.

The temptation to use these kinds of intimidation tactics must be guarded against vigilantly. The threat or use of physical force will destroy the home as a safe haven for your child. Deprogram your tendency to intimidate, for it breeds either aggression or excessive passivity in response. You create either a bully or a soul fearful of going out into the world. Be careful of your body language as well. Your tone of voice, your eyes, your whole energy can disturb your child. The father's position involves protecting his child and teaching his child to live safely in the world. If this isn't accomplished—if a child fears the father and finds no way to bond with him—a separation is created between father and child that may never be repaired. In past generations, it was common to hit children—and unfortunately in some homes it still is (though that practice has decreased). But not all violence is physical; it can be verbal and emotional too—and these are just as devastating. Worse, violence breeds violence. When you resort to it as a tactic, you're teaching your children that it's okay to use force when someone is misbehaving.

The new souls you help come to this earth must be free to take their journeys safely. Our responsibility is to love and protect them and teach them to be safe in this world. Our job is to listen to our children, learn a new receptivity. To defy this by invalidating or violating the soul of a child stands as the most horrible of crimes. If you've found yourself doing anything less than giving pure love, respect, and compassion, it's time to look deep within and change your course. Break the negative cycle that you've inherited and hold onto the positive. Seek to cultivate growth and nurturing behavior, and you'll be doing all you can to help create balanced, healthy souls who'll take their journeys here in a peaceful, loving world.

THREE

❧ *Arrival*

For nine months your child has been developing. Now he or she is ready to leave the womb and come out naked into the world. This is the arrival, the moment when you first set your eyes on God's miracle, the moment when you hear that first breath and touch every part of that beautiful body that you helped to create. If fate or faith hands you a newborn through adoption, the arrival is still an incredibly glorious experience. You now can hold a tiny human being in your hands and behold the beauty of little arms, legs, hands, feet, nose, mouth, eyes, ears, spine—not to mention the little tush. "Oh, my

God!" you think: you're holding what you'll be responsible for almost the rest of your life. The universe has given you the ultimate responsibility: to raise, love, protect, and teach this soul that's chosen you.

When Maximo first came home, I needed more help than most mothers probably find they need. I was so physically unwell from the botched treatment I'd received from the attending doctor that I had to hire a woman to help me. I ended up asking the baby nurse I'd tired for the first few days home to stay longer. She was a godsend: with her aid, I could give Maximo all the pure love and focus he needed from his mom. I couldn't walk around with him or do stand-up tasks such as changing his diapers; I could only hold him in bed. A baby, when he or she first comes home, needs 100 percent of your love and attention. This is the time when your whole life should be geared to the needs and wants of your baby. Now that this little soul is completely in the body here on earth, making him or her feel as comfortable and welcome as you can is your number-one priority.

How do you live up to that ultimate responsibility?

This chapter has a dual purpose. It gives practical suggestions about making this new soul welcome in the world; in addition, it discusses how to communicate the full depth of your love to the little being you've helped to create and how to rely on your own intuition about providing this new being with everything it needs. Now especially, with the arrival of your child, you must make sure that needed protective boundaries are in place.

Indeed, your first priority is to create a protection zone for your newborn. People often want to give what they think is loving advice about what you should and shouldn't be doing as a new parent. Their advice can overwhelm you, keeping you from tapping into your own intuitive power. Explain to friends and relatives that you need "alone time," that in these early days you'd be grateful if they'd give you and your child time to allow your newfound positive energy to flow. You need to protect yourself and your newborn from over-stimulation.

Overstimulation can be particularly hard to limit when it comes in the form of well-intended cooing and oohing-and-aahing from doting aunts, cousins, grand-mothers, and next-door neighbors. Even though these well-meaning friends and relatives may feel all the love in the world for your infant, hours of exposure to unfa-miliar faces and sounds is exhausting and confusing to your baby and to you. When you overstimulate your newborn by keeping him or her in an unpeaceful environment too long (at a party, in a room with loud music, or in circumstances that prevent a nap when a nap is needed), you create many problems for your child and for yourself. This doesn't mean that you should never involve your infant in a happy gathering or party: parties can be fun, and the positive energy in the room can be wonderfully nurturing to both you and your infant. But at first your little baby can take only very small doses of this kind of lively activity.

It's hard enough for adults to recover from over-stimulation; just imagine the negative effect it has on a fragile baby! In adults it creates overtiredness, anxiety, and a restlessness that can take a long time to work out of our systems. When people go to parties that run late into the night, they sometimes find it hard to get to sleep; even if they simply fall out from the exhaustion, the next day is almost always a killer. They're run-down, tired, and unable to function well. With their resistance down, they can easily catch a cold or a cough or anything else floating around. During the days it takes to get well again, they realize that they brought it all on themselves—because of overstimulation.

How could helpless children or infants ward all this off? They try with naps, but they're at the mercy of their parents' judgment. It's *you* who is ultimately responsible for making sure your child isn't overstimulated. The old theory of keeping newborns in loud places to teach them to sleep more deeply is ridiculous if not malicious. Each soul that comes here is an individual. Some sleep more deeply than others, but all newborns deserve the respect of being granted some quiet time; they need peace and tranquillity to develop freely. Your baby depends completely upon you to create a peaceful environment. When you go to a four-hour family function full of music, laughter, and loudness, think of your newborn, call it a day while the get-together is still in full swing, and return to a peaceful, safe, comfortable place so that your child and you can relax. If you choose to remain in an overstimulating environment, most likely your newborn will have a difficult time sleeping soundly through that night; furthermore, he or she may be very restless the next day. Create balance in your newborn's life and peace in his or her surrounding environment, and your child will be one step closer to enjoying a lifetime of balance and tranquillity.

Creating a healthy environment for your newborn can't stop when you're not around. If for some reason you can't spend time with your newborn due to work or other obligations and someone else is helping you care for him or her—a baby-sitter, housekeeper, or child-care worker—set your boundaries with that person too. Explain clearly just what you expect from your baby's caretaker. Your newborn's development doesn't stop when you're not there. The best thing you can do is direct the caretaker with positive energy and strength. Explain how you want the caretaker to act, how you want your child's needs met. Your instincts must provide guidance. If you and your caretaker share the same instincts, wonderful— but if they're not the same, your law is law. If you can't be physically present with your newborn, toddler, or child of any age, at least you're there in spirit, with strong direction. Too many mothers leave their children with a caretaker whose instincts and ideas differ from their own. This can only breed confusion for a child, who hasn't yet learned to interpret mixed messages.

As infants, we arrive in this world after spending nine months in a warm, dark, secure place. When we arrive, we're suddenly out in the open light, in a harsh and cold environment. The need for our caretakers to hold us and keep us warm is tremendously strong. Their response to our need lays the foundation for all we learn about trust and safety. In the past, some believed that too much tenderness, too much attentiveness, would create a spoiled child. Your own heart will probably tell you how wrong and negative this old belief is. Allowing yourself such negative thoughts isn't only a waste of time and energy, it's also harmful to your child.

If you hear yourself thinking, "If I hold him a lot, he'll want it more," ask yourself, "Is that my instinct or something I heard or read somewhere?" This replaying of negative ideas—and adherence to them—is what has created the chaos in people's lives today. How can anyone know what each individual soul will do with love? We know only how individuals behave when denied love. When you hold back caring for your child, nurturing your child, and attending to your child's needs, you hold back love. Let your heart and soul guide you. Your child needs to feel your loving presence—as much of it as you can give. There's no such thing as too much love.

Attending to your newborn's needs immediately isn't the act of an obsessive parent; it's an act of love and understanding. In responding immediately and lovingly, you'll be telling the soul in your care that you understand that he or she is helpless right now in life and can trust you to be there. You'll also be teaching your child the true meaning of safety, trust, and comfort—the very things so many of us crave and search for. Just think of lying in the crib helpless, without the ability to get out or even the muscle to move around or turn over. Think of soiling your pants and not being able to change them, desperately needing help. Then imagine that the one you trust decides that you should cry a little while longer, stay in your distress, because someone told him or her that's what a parent should do. *Never* let your child's cries go unanswered. Would you like to cry for someone at any age and be ignored? What you're saying to your child with a hold-back stance is, "I don't care!" Respond to your child's cry, for it's his or her only means of communication with you, of letting you know you're needed.

It's true that when we're older (starting at about age five or six), crying becomes an outlet to release our anguish; and at that point we may need to be left alone to cry so that we can sort out our feelings. The parent who moves in too quickly to "fix" the older child can interfere with this necessary solitude. When they're ready, older children will generally let you know when they need to be comforted.

But infants don't yet have these inner resources; their cries need your attention. When you first come home with your newborn, he or she needs you full-time. This life is just as new to him or her as it is to you. We don't need to pretend that because we're adults we need to be in control or have all the answers. Tell your newborn when and if you're not sure of what you're doing. Maintain the bridge of communication that you started when you first learned you were pregnant. When you're feeling uncertain, talking may help you to figure it out, but if you don't communicate, your child feels rejection. He or she can hear you and feel you—and will reward you with love if you respect him or her as an individual equal to you. Talk to this soul you've brought to life, and listen as your new arrival talks back to you, through sounds, expressions, and the movement of those little limbs.

As I noted earlier, you're always on safe ground when you begin by living in the moment, keeping all of your attention focused on the present, letting your feelings and instincts guide your actions. Don't miss the moment. Don't live in the future, worrying about what might happen, dreaming of what could be. Stay focused on yourself and what you're feeling for your newborn right now. Listen for your newborn's needs and respond the way your heart and soul encourage you to respond, not how your mother, sister, friends, doctor, or parenting book of yesteryear tells you to respond. Though all may give some sound advice, follow your own loving instincts first. If your baby is crying and you want to hold him or her, that's instinct. Do it—and do it for as long as you want.

There are so many ways to let your baby know you're "with" him or her—that you're in harmony with your baby's soul. Repeating sounds, for example, is a wonderful confirmation that you're listening to your infant. It also reinforces your newborn's ability to use specific muscles to reach those tones. However, don't limit yourself to nonsense sounds; don't make the mistake of making only goo-goo ga-ga sounds to your newborn. Baby talk is cute, no doubt, and the first attempts at vocal communication by a child are as beautiful as any melody. But talk normally to your new arrival as well. Let your child know how happy you are that he or she is finally here. Talk of your feelings—tell your newborn every day how much you love him or her—because if you don't, your baby can feel only your energy, both positive and negative. Without your loving words, babies don't always understand what you're trying to communicate, and the resulting confusion can be detrimental to a child's healthy emotional development.

Have you ever heard someone say to a parent, "Why are you talking to your baby like that? He doesn't understand you"? Be skeptical of such a judgment. There's no scientific information about how much a child absorbs from normal adult conversation. Your newborn heard and understood you in the womb, and he or she will understand you, at some level, now. Talk to your newborn simply and clearly. Have great conversations with him or her. Remember that I said Michael would discuss finances with Maximo even when he was in the womb? After Maximo came home, as he grew from infant to baby to toddler, he frequently watched his dad working at a big desk. He knew this was Michael's *domain*. Now, when Michael travels and calls Maximo from out of town, Maximo takes the call at Michael's desk—announcing the fact with pride to his father: "I'm at your desk, Dad. I'm going through your things. I'm taking care of business while you're away!" Maximo loves all the papers on that desk; he wants his dad to know that even when he's away, somebody is at the helm. Some of this began back in the womb, when Michael first lovingly talked about finances to Max's growing soul. It continued after Maximo came home: I'd bring the infant Maximo to his dad's desk, and he'd watch wonderingly while Michael paid our bills. Never think, when your newborn is near, that you're alone. You're closer than you can imagine to the best friend you'll ever know.

It's important to be aware not only of what you tell your child but also of the messages you give yourself. How you handle yourself on your new journey, how you adjust to being a mother or father, is as important as how you handle your newborn. Tell yourself, "Life has changed for the better." If you plant a fearful and negative message in your head—"Oh, my God, what have I done? I don't have a moment to myself!"—you'll begin to resent your newborn, invalidating your child's very existence. In the beginning, there's no question that you won't have much time for yourself. Accept this as a necessary part of the pact you've made with the new, helpless soul in your care. Take some of the focus off your superficial self and put it onto what truly makes you who you are. Your preparenting focus may have been on our job, your hair, your clothes, your car, your home, or any number of equally superficial things that you thought defined you. But bringing another human being into this world (or adopting another human being) and giving that child love, respect, and compassion, allowing that child to take his or her journey individually (not the way you or anyone else thinks the journey should be), are the most wonderful gifts you can give to your child. You're the power that can give these gifts; that's who you *are*. Give freely—then enjoy every moment spent with your new arrival.

The lessons you learn from the very first day you bring your baby home will serve you later on as well:

trusting your own intuition, staying in the moment, appreciating the fact that your child is an individual with his or her own personality, talents, and likes and dislikes. These lessons give birth to healthy attitudes that will help you to navigate subsequent stages in the baby's and toddler's development—talking, walking, using the toilet, and getting along with other kids.

It isn't important how much faster your neighbor's or friend's child develops than yours. Don't push your child into anything. Your child has a mind of his own and deserves to develop his talents in his own time. You can suggest to your child at around two or three years that it would be nice to drink out of a cup; you can show her how to do it; you can buy some fun cups to get her started. But if she isn't ready to let go of her bottle, don't force the issue. A very wise mother once said, "Have you ever seen someone walk down the aisle with a bottle?" Eventually the child will make the shift—but let her make it in her own time. The same applies to sleeping, diapers, and walking. We can help a child to get on some kind of schedule of sleep, but we can't *force* a child to sleep. We can't *demand* that he or she sleep. Such a charge could create a very nervous child. Don't you find that your own sleep pattern changes from time to time, even if most of the time you're on a regular schedule? Well, the same will happen for your child.

As for coming out of diapers: you can present underwear to your child and explain what it's for and why it's the next step, but forcing your child to wear it is ridiculous. Sitting in the bathroom forcing your child to use the toilet, or intimidating him by saying that everyone else wears underwear, is disrespectful of your child's individuality. Buy some nice underwear, give it to him, suggest that he put it away in his room, and tell him that when he's ready to wear it, you'll be there to help. Allow your child to make these choices and you'll be helping to create a very stable soul, one who understands and takes pride in his or her own individuality and accomplishments.

And how about walking? First-time parents often don't understand that they need to get ready to lose ten pounds once their little one walks! Don't look at your wonderful child as developing late or think she's slow if she doesn't walk when you think it's time. Your baby will turn over in the crib when the time is right; your child will crawl when she's ready; your toddler will drink out of a cup, wear underwear, walk, and talk when the time is right. (If you notice a truly abnormal delay in development, however, you should of course consult your doctor.)

Your patience is the supreme virtue in these early years, and your understanding is also important. If you allow your newborn to ease into each stage, it will be easier for you, not to mention easier and healthier for your child. Remember: don't allow pressures from outside your boundaries to reach your new arrival. You must *act*, not *react*. Acting is living in the moment, allowing every tiny advance to be an interesting, fun step into life.

Nothing you've ever experienced in life compares to the moment of arrival. Nothing you've ever held in your hands feels like the soft skin and tiny body of your child, whose wondering eyes look to you for guidance, safety, and love. And love is what you'll receive in return. But you must learn to let go of what you want the future to hold for your child. Enjoy the arrival, and know that there are many more "arrivals" to come in your baby's life. Welcome each one, and let the future take care of itself.

FOUR

❧ *Siblings*

Most families have more than one child. In most Western countries, the average family includes two to four children. It's normal for each new arrival to produce both positive and negative feelings in the family. The new baby's brothers and sisters may feel joy that another child has come into their home but may also fear that the new family member will take the parents' love and attention away from them. While some degree of competition between siblings is normal, it's the parents' task to keep the balance of peace and happiness between and among their children. The goal of parents of this and coming generations is to eliminate destructive sibling rivalry—to make it clear that every child in the family is special and deserves the parents' unconditional love and acceptance. Through loving examples and tender guidance, respect, and compassion, parents can teach children to respect each other's individuality and promote harmony and support for each member of the family.

When a newborn arrives in a family that's already blessed with a child (or children), loving parents must remember not to elevate the new and diminish the already-arrived souls. Adding to your family gracefully is the key to keeping love in balance. Pressuring older children into feeling they must at once understand this new soul is ultimately harmful to the process of acceptance. We can't *create* the bonds of love between any other two people; it simply isn't our place. Let your children's journeys ease into one another by explaining to older offspring that they now have a brother or sister and letting them discover each other on their own and in their own ways. Telling them they *have* to love one another is like setting up an arranged marriage. Give the children time to discover themselves and each other. They'll very likely become inseparable—but even if they don't, they'll grow to respect and admire each other for the different people they are.

Siblings need to be left on their own with each other to learn to share themselves lovingly. The process begins with mothers and fathers teaching children what it means to share each other, to accept and respect the individuality of another person. Healthy competition exists when each sibling asserts his or her own individuality in a positive way—each celebrating the other's differences. Sibling rivalry is about sabotage and negativity, vengefulness and vindictiveness. Teaching children—and allowing them to teach themselves—to respect and accept each other's individual journeys and differences creates enormous harmony. Forcing conformity to someone else's ideas creates a chaotic imbalance in an individual's life.

When a mother asks her daughter why she can't be like her brother or sister, or when a father speaks ill of one sibling to another, it's the beginning of the end of a healthy, loving sibling relationship. Negative thoughts about siblings are injected into the children's psyches, and the rivalry begins. A child's mind rationalizes that because the parents are the authority figures, they must be right. A child might think, "My mother thinks less of my brother than of me. Why should I feel anything more about him than she does?" Or "My father thinks less of my sister, so I don't like her either."

We're not sharing each other lovingly when we speak ill of anyone—especially of our own children. It's most important that you don't favor (or even appear to favor) one child over another. When a new child is brought home, parents need to consider the older sibling's feelings. The older siblings are as special and as important as the new arrival, and they must not be cast aside or *forced* to love their new sibling. In time, if they're allowed to get to know one another freely, without being told how they should feel about each other, siblings will develop their own bond; and that bond will be stronger than anything built by force or coercion. There's no timetable governing the coming-together and the parting of siblings, however. When siblings aren't allowed to connect freely early on, a true connection sometimes still happens much later in life. One friend of mine, younger by six years than his older brother, says that as kids they were always bickering and that their age difference was just too great for them ever to feel like "equals." But after the younger brother graduated college, he got in touch again with his older brother, and he was amazed by how much they now had in common. "It was like discovering I had more family than I thought I had," he told me. These brothers confirm the tenet that siblings need to work out their own relationships with each other.

If care isn't taken to share love equally among children, jealousy breeds, creating a lifelong battle between siblings. Sometimes this happens because one child is temperamentally more like the parent or parents than the other, and the sibling who differs feels left out. When Zoe, Marilyn's daughter and Max's friend, does something really wonderful and I respond lovingly, Max often feels jealous; he has a tendency to say, "You hate me." My first impulse is to say (a bit brusquely), "Of *course* I love you; don't be silly!" But Max needs more that this abrupt reassurance (which isn't very reassuring after all); he needs to see that when Zoë does something wonderful, he and I *both* can be happy about it. There's more than enough love to share among the three of us. We need to take care, though, not to pay more attention to the child who's more like us, who more closely shares our interests than another son or daughter. The wounds of feeling bad because you don't share your sibling's or parent's talents or interests can be devastating. As I was growing up, I wasn't nearly as interested in school as my sister was. She possessed a scholastic intelligence; I possessed an emotional intelligence. My mind needed to be fed in a different way from hers, which unfortunately created an extraordinary division between us, with me on the losing end in the family. Emotional intelligence— the power of intuition and empathy, the ability to understand feelings—wasn't valued in my family. (As I said at the outset, my mother had a good deal of innate emotional intelligence, which she recognized that I in turn inherited from her. But she mistrusted it, was afraid of it—saw it far more as an affliction than as a blessing.) My father was like my sister, and it was clear he preferred her over me because of her academic interests. He could identify with her more easily. And because my mother feared her emotional intelligence, she channeled it negatively, causing her feelings to be bottled up. As I've said, when I was born my mother fell into a deep postpartum depression. My sister, bolstered by feeling validated by our father in her interests and temperament, gave voice to the message my whole family gave me from the moment I arrived on the scene: "Mommy was okay before you came along." My whole family blamed my mother's depression—a depression that she never came out of—on my birth.

Parents need to guard against siding with one child against any of their other children. My niece, Sara, once felt very jealous of my special spiritual relationship with my nephew, Seth. More scholastically oriented than either Seth or I, she once felt that this was an unbridgeable gap between us; she felt that I preferred Seth because he was more like me. (She shared this with me in a phone call from college.) But I told Sara, "I treasure my connection to you every bit as much as the one I have with Seth. I've always been awed by your scholastic abilities. I love listening to you—there's so much you teach me!" Our differences don't mean that we can't communicate; rather, they give us the opportunity to teach each other more about our different perspectives. I let her know how much I admire her logical stance. There's no reason for her to be jealous of Seth, because our connection is fully as wonderful—just in a different way.

The seeds of jealousy are planted by negatively comparing your children to each other—a spiteful comparison that almost always blossoms into dysfunction later on. Hate crops up early in the life of a child subjected to frequent comparison—even if he or she is the one favorably compared—and that child must battle the hate for the rest of his or her life. These angry, jealous souls may be difficult to live with or even spend time with; these invalidated souls often become tricksters, manipulators. Outwardly they may act friendly, but inwardly they often boil with resentment and anger, wasting their time in negative thoughts of sabotage, losing sight of their own journey while trying to throw others off theirs. Siblings who have felt acceptance and love in their family glide through their life without disrupting anyone else's.

These are the souls who make wonderful brothers and sisters, friends, husbands, or wives—and, most important, loving moms and dads.

Parents can do much to keep jealous rivalries from overcoming their children by consciously fighting every urge to place their children in opposition to each other. Once again, you may have to review the positive and negative aspects of your own sibling relationships to increase this consciousness—to be on the lookout for those times when, by an old reflex, you may be about to compare your children to one another—to one's favor and the other's disadvantage. You may simply be repeating your own history without realizing it, repeating a setup in which your parents compared you to your own brother or sister. From conception, the new soul entering the gateway hears its parents talk about its siblings (if there are any). If the talk is negative, it creates an imbalance throughout the child's life. The progression might go as follows: "It was easier to carry your brother. I wasn't sick with him. The birth was easier." Or "Your sister learned to sleep through the night faster than you. You stopped the bottle before she did. You read books before your sister. Your sister was out of diapers before you." Comparing one child to another, holding one up as better than the other, causes anger and resentment that continue into both siblings' adult lives. When the children have grown into adults, many parents think nothing of calling one child to speak badly of the other. Such attempts to win one sibling to the side of the parents reopens or reinforces any negative feelings that one sibling has for the other.

If you have a problem with your child, it's your duty as a parent and a loving human being to deal with it directly. People who talk ill of others do so because they weren't taught how to confront their feelings openly. Learn to deal openly with your children, respecting their points of view, and they'll learn to deal openly with each other. This will also teach them compassion: the understanding that we can still love each other even when we disagree. Ultimately, this will bring them closer to their siblings and to you, rather than set them in opposing camps.

Once again: be careful not to replay with your own children negative patterns that may have existed between you and your own siblings. You may find, as your mother and father found, that one of your children reflects you more than another. Guard against what may have been done to you: show the child who's different from you that you value and love him or her as much as his or her brothers and sisters. Be curious about the "different" child: he or she may have much to teach you. Bring a sense of awe, wonder, and mystery to the child you don't understand.

You can continue to learn about sibling relationships by paying attention to your own ongoing connections to brothers and sisters and by analyzing the effects of your upbringing on all of you. Sometimes, unfortunately, you may discover that you can't connect even now— that the differences between you, or the resentments one or both of you still hold, are for the moment insurmountable. Sadly, my sister and I have come to this kind of impasse; she's never healed from negativity instilled in her by our parents. But even while there's now no point of contact between us, I still respect her journey. I've learned to let go and allow both of us to evolve in the ways we each must.

If you find yourself fighting other people's wars, it's time to stop. If you've been judging your sibling by standards your parents placed in your mind, if you've been fighting your parents' wars with your sibling, then you'll never know your sibling as an individual, never respect his or her own journey. Worse, you'll unconsciously bring the same unhappy fate to your own children. Try focusing on what was positive between you: any moment in your life in which you and your sibling supported each other, showed each other love, gives you a model to keep in mind as you deal with your own children. Some amount of competition is probably inevitable. But competition that sprouts up momentarily between the siblings themselves is generally a lot less damaging than competition bred, over years, by parents. Focus on the wonderful camaraderie brothers and sisters can know. Do everything you can to foster a positive, loving, free connection between your children. We need to consider their birth order as well. Middle children often feel lost in the crowd; firstborns tend to feel a good deal of pressure to succeed, and resentment at younger siblings who take away attention from them; and youngest children may want to be "the baby" for longer than is healthy. Be conscious of these natural feelings, fears, and resentments, and do what you can to counter them, reassuring and encouraging a shy middle child, giving your youngest a bit more responsibility, comforting your oldest child by showing how much you love him or her. There's much that parents can do to heal the natural rifts and occasional resentments and rivalries that occur in families with more than one child.

Respect your own brothers' and sisters' journeys as you learn to respect your children's. Teach unconditional love by positive example. Seek never to violate or invalidate their souls. Strive for honesty in sharing your feelings directly with your loved ones, but share with one another in the most positive, loving way. If we can begin to teach our new souls love and respect for one another, we can create for them a stable basis for living their own individual journeys.

Parents can avoid creating sibling rivalry by never expecting older children to be responsible for their younger siblings without giving them the choice. It's ultimately damaging to their relationship to force the issue. If they're respected from birth by being given reasonable choices, they'll be happy to give and help. Most of the time responsibility is assigned to the older child without choice very early in life, creating resentment in the relationship—especially on the part of the older sibling. Say, for example, that you and your older son and younger daughter are outside playing in the yard when the phone rings. Saying to your son, "I need to go into the house, so you must watch your sister," won't be nearly as nurturing and effective as saying, "Do you think you could watch your sister for me for a few minutes until I come back outside?" That second communication gives respect and love by making it your child's choice to say, "Yes, I can," or "No, I don't want to." But you have to be willing to accept the answer. Demanding a yes could put your younger child in danger of not being watched carefully. Given the choice, most of the time your children will be happy to help both you and their siblings—especially when it seems to be a team effort involving all of you, an effort in which they have a voice that counts. The magic here is offering a choice. It lets a child know that you feel he or she is capable not only of taking care of a younger child but also of making a decision.

Some children might want to look after their siblings; others might not. It's a matter of personality. Some children are natural caretakers; others are natural loners. Every child develops a different personality. We come here with our souls and the journey our souls must take. Our personalities develop later, as we begin to take those journeys. We're taught about race, religion, bad and good behavior, judgment, prejudice, and so on; and from these "lessons," our personalities develop. Because my sister and I don't get along well, we communicate no more than we absolutely have to. Nonetheless, her children—Seth and Sara—are, as I've said, a very important part of my family's life. In addition, Max has always felt close to their housekeeper, Gloria, a black woman from Trinidad. One day when Seth and Sara were coming over, Max asked if their mother was coming too. I was taken aback—what did he mean? He surely couldn't have expected my sister, whom he'd rarely seen. "You know, their *mother,*" he said—"Gloria." Max lacked any sense that because Gloria was black it was unlikely she was Seth and Sara's mother. His utter lack of prejudice made it stunningly clear that prejudice is *learned* (and that, thank God, Max hadn't learned it).

Allow each of your children the freedom to develop his or her own personality, rather than forcing them to adopt yours. Give them the freedom to have clear, good intentions when it comes to their siblings and the world around them. Negative sibling rivalry will still sometimes crop up, but through love and respect you can keep it to a minimum. Always verbally express support and love of your children to them when their siblings are around. Confirm their choices to their siblings with positive, loving approval. You may not agree with the choices your children make, but their journeys are their own; you can't expect them to do things your way, for only their *own* way is right for them.

This sometimes means letting go of deeply entrenched assumptions and expectations. My nephew is now in his early twenties; I've always loved and regarded Seth as one of my own children—sometimes as my brother—and empathized with his pain at having disappointed his own family by dropping out of college to pursue a career in the culinary arts. But sad as I was that his decision caused resentment and unhappiness in his own family, I was proud and thrilled for him that he nonetheless decided to pursue his own journey. Recently, after meditating, I had a prophetic dream about Seth—a dream that I knew applied to so many others as well. A voice told me, "Plunge forward, without looking back. Only in the bizarre lies your future." Sara, who at first sided a bit with the rest of her family in not understanding or supporting her brother's choice, has slowly come around as she's seen how much this career decision means to Seth. She's found, by trusting in her love for her brother, a way to understand and connect with him, even if it means disagreeing with the rest of her family. Often siblings who support each other even in the face of parental opposition find that their sibling bond can give them more of a sense of "family" than they ever experienced with their parents.

Sometimes the choices our siblings or children make may seem to us "bizarre," but we need to respect and celebrate the fact that they know where they must go. We must applaud them for the courage and work they exhibit in following the path that's necessary for them, even if that path is very different from our own. Doing this can bring family members so much closer.

This applies equally to your children's sexuality. Children who become gay adults, for example, are making a soul choice that's necessary for them. (By *soul choice* I mean a choice made by the soul before birth—made to teach certain lessons in the coming life.) Don't judge, hate, or be afraid of their differences. You can respect what you don't understand and love your children with all your heart, whatever choices they may feel compelled to make.

Not all siblings are biological brothers and sisters. Somehow "only children," as they undertake their spiritual journeys, often come across spiritual siblings, sometimes early in their lives, sometimes much later on. These spiritual siblings seem to know from the moment they meet each other that they share a deep, abiding bond. Maximo has a spiritual sibling in Zoe, for example—who, as I've mentioned, is the child of one of my dearest friends and was born a year (to the day) before Maximo. Spiritual siblings are connected in a different, more intimate sense than friends are. Friends are often people whose approval you seek, so you respect their boundaries and restrict your own behavior somewhat. There are fewer boundaries between siblings—even siblings of the spiritual variety: being a brother or sister seems to give you license to tread over the edges of these boundaries, sometimes even to hurt each other. Thus the sibling relationship offers a very special and powerful intimacy. From the moment they laid eyes on each other, Zoë and Maximo experienced this intimacy. They quickly became inseparable. It's fascinating to watch them work out their relationship as they grow older.

Sometimes when they disagree—for example, squabbling over sharing a toy—it can sound terrible to us parents. My first impulse is often to intervene and restore peace. But this isn't always a good idea. As I've suggested, parents need to learn to give their children and their biological or spiritual siblings the chance to work out their differences themselves. Parents must, of course, also understand that toddlers do sometimes need to be separated; the very young are too small, too immature, to work out all of their differences themselves. But making the attempt is an important learning experience—one that teaches them how to resolve disagreements in the rest of their relationships and in life. Furthermore, the renewed bond that comes from siblings working out problems on their own can create an even stronger love, intimacy, and respect between them. Once again, there's no timetable here: differences may take months, years, or even decades to work out. It's up to the siblings—not the parents. Even when we're older, we must not allow our parents to cause dissension between us and our siblings.

Remember that your children's choices guide them to the very lessons they came here to learn. Siblings who learn to respect each other's choices do more than pave the way to a more loving bond with each other. They may also give themselves permission to follow secret dreams or desires by applauding decisions their brothers and sisters have made to follow difficult or uncharted paths. In this sense, one sibling can help another by signaling, "See? It's okay: I'm doing what I need to. You can do what *you* need to do too!"

One of your responsibilities in your journey as a parent involves teaching your children love, respect, compassion, and safety here on earth. Respecting their individual souls and journeys, and teaching them to respect each other's, is the pathway to harmony and peace for your family. You have the power to create a home and family free from dysfunction and despair. Stay focused on this beautiful part of your journey, and you'll succeed in creating a happier, healthier, and safer world for your children to take their own journeys in.

FIVE

↔ *Communication*

We've already talked about the amazing depth and range of communication possible between mothers, fathers, and the souls of our children. Even as the soul manifests in the womb before birth, the principles of communicating openly and honestly enable you to emphasize the positive by expressing abundant love. This remains as important after birth as during pregnancy. But the grace of carrying out this communication, once you're faced with a physical one-on-one presence, requires more skill. Your sounds, words, and gestures are more complicated now that your infant is in your arms.

Your tone—especially before your baby learns to understand words—is just as important as the content of your communication. You need to communicate as much love as you can, as often as you can, with touch and with the sound of your voice. You communicate much more to your child, before and after birth, than you realize, and there's no way of telling what he or she will or will not understand. You need to make every encounter you have with your child as loving, reassuring, and attentive to his or her needs as possible. Look at your baby's face and body language; allow yourself to sense what your baby may not be able to tell you in language but is trying to communicate to you through other means. If you've connected with your baby's soul before birth, you'll have paved the way to this sensitivity now that your baby is in the world. Even before children have language, they have many things to tell you as they respond to and absorb more of their environment. Pay attention to your baby's subtlest facial expressions and littlest gestures, and listen with your heart.

When your infant grows to the toddler stage and begins to use language, a new and larger world is opened up. Your child can now tell you more about his or her feelings and desires, frustrations and needs. You need to keep your own communication to your child as simple and truthful as possible. Holding back an explanation because you don't feel like expressing your emotions or because "I'm the father [or mother] and don't need to give you an explanation" is unfair of you. Respecting your child's thought processes and need for clear explanations is a vital key to raising him or her. The continuation of this respect will create a lifetime of closeness between you and your child.

We create dysfunction in our children's lives when we invalidate who they are and what they say or do by predetermining what they ought to be feeling, thinking, and doing. In this cast of mind, we simply dismiss anything about them of which we don't approve: if they don't adhere to our preconceptions, they're "wrong." Another even more slippery problem arises when you, as the parent, think that you see clearly the situation your child is facing, and you want to give your perspective—immediately—so that your child will see it your way. That simply doesn't work, however. You have to wait for your children—indeed, for everyone in your life—to see it their own way.

Invalidation creates insecurity in your child's mind and imbalance in your child's soul. By not explaining to your child as much as you can, by holding back your feelings and thoughts, you're sending the message that he isn't equal to you as a human being. Think back on the discussion, in our chapter on fathers, of how powerful the word *no* is. When you say simply, "No, because I said so," you're telling your child that he doesn't deserve an explanation. But children more than deserve that explanation; they *need* it to understand, to grow, and in some cases to stay safe in the world. Your child need not agree with your explanation—often he won't—but he deserves to know the reasons behind your actions, just as you deserve to know the reasons behind his. In communicating with your child, open up with questions that can help him to think about the reality of the moment. "What do you think you should . . . ?" is an excellent way to teach children communication skills and responsibility—helping them to think for themselves rather than just follow orders.

Maximo woke up recently and announced he didn't want to go to school. "I don't feel good," he complained. I might have said, "Don't make excuses! You have to go to school whether you want to go or not!" But whether or not Maximo didn't feel good physically, he was telling me the truth. He didn't feel good emotionally. I asked him, "What hurts?" He said, "I have a stomachache." A small child doesn't always know what he's feeling—or even exactly where his stomach is. So I asked, "Where does it hurt?" He touched his heart. I commiserated with him that stomachaches were no fun. Then I changed tactics. "You have so many friends at school whom you'll miss and who will miss you," I said with a sigh. I started to talk to him about the fun parts of school, the joy it brings him. His eyes brightened as he remembered those fun and joyous parts himself. "Maybe my stomachache isn't so bad," he said. I allowed him the time to change his own mind, to decide for himself that he wanted to go to school. The important thing is that I didn't dismiss anything Maximo told me. I showed him that I respected his point of view. Then I offered my own point of view. The child placed in this situation is made to think, reason, and come up with an answer on his own. You can help him by providing guidance and suggesting options rather than giving orders. In your child's eyes, you become a safe parent to communicate with.

What about dealing with fears—such as those regarding the bogeyman, the dragon in the closet, the monster under the bed? Or "real" fears your child may hear about on television? Recently Max and I had to take a plane trip from Florida to New Jersey. Max had flown many times before with no problem. Shortly before this trip, however, there had been a terrible plane

crash in the Everglades that no one on board had sur-
vived, reports of which we couldn't escape on television
and the car radio. Maximo suddenly got very frightened
of flying. He looked at me with wide eyes and asked me,
point-blank, "What happens when you go into the water
after the plane crashes?" My first impulse was to reassure him: "Our plane won't crash, honey. Don't worry."
But he wasn't appeased. "*What happens,*" he repeated
with a strong, insistent voice, "when you go into the
water?" I now knew he really wanted an answer. I explained that if the plane did crash—which there was
very little chance of its doing—we'd all have warning to
put on our lifejackets and follow the crew's instructions.
Maximo now had a reasonable answer to his reasonable
question. When I took him seriously, I validated him.
And I allowed him, once again, to come to his own
peace with my answer.

When you explain anything to your children, stay
focused on the truth. *Truth* is a big word, and an even
bigger responsibility. Holding back and not communicating will bind and enslave your soul and the souls of
your children; on the other hand, as the well-known saying goes, the truth will always set you free. If you start
early—from the very beginning—with the truth, your
children will be honest souls, and they, as well as you,

will be free. When we stay clear with our children, communicating truthfully with them about why things are the way they are, they'll feel clearer themselves about why they're doing whatever it is they're doing in their lives. What exactly *is* the truth? The truth is what's happening in the moment. The truth is reality, not fiction. The truth is how we feel, not how we're supposed to feel. And in truth there's strength.

A simple, good example of explaining the truth to your child involves bedtime. When your baby or youngster is crying and won't go to bed, no matter how old she is, explain calmly why she *needs* to go to bed. Explain to her that it's nighttime, most of us sleep at night, and sleep is part of health. You may not get her to bed at that moment, but if you never tell her *why*, choosing instead to force the issue with "I said so, and that's final," you'll create a fear of sleep and maybe even a feeling of punishment associated with sleep. Have patience. Some little souls fight it to the end, and some just go to sleep. But either way, your open, loving communication with your child is the most important aspect.

Children always know when you're lying to them. This means you have to be truthful not only about why people need to go to bed, or what happens when airplanes crash, but about your own life. One of the worst things parents can do is keep a dark secret in the closet about their lives. Can you recognize that principle in the following scenario? As an adult, you remember that your uncle was divorced and your cousins were awarded to your uncle, not your aunt, who went into a hospital never to be seen again. As a child, all you heard was that your aunt was put away and your cousins—those poor, poor children—had to live a miserable life with their father. You were never told anything more; your family simply never spoke about it. But matters such as these *need* to be spoken of. When you were old enough to understand the basics, you deserved to know that your aunt had a chemical imbalance and needed medical care, and that your cousins were happy living with their loving dad. You would have realized that you had a sick aunt and that your cousins were pretty lucky to have such a good father, instead of believing that you had some weirdo aunt and poor, miserable cousins who would never be happy again. Holding back the truth from children in this way creates that much more pain in the future. In addition, it may instill irrational fears (for example, as in this case, a fear of going into the hospital: Will you ever come out, or will you be locked up forever as your aunt was?).

Think back on your childhood. How well did your parents communicate with you? Are you simply passing on dysfunctional habits to your children? Sometimes, because these habits are so reflexive, it can be very hard not to. Recently Maximo had a whiny day. He was dissatisfied with everything. It felt to me as if he wanted to torture me: nothing was good enough; I never did what he wanted me to or got him what he wanted to have when he wanted to have it. I had the impulse to floor him—scream and yell at him for misbehaving—or just send him to his room.

But had I done that, I would have been ignoring the real issue. What was up with him? Why was he so upset? I decided to answer him differently. When he kept repeating, "I want what I want, and I want it now!" I calmly explained that nothing I did was making him happy and that this wasn't fair to me. I took deep breaths and reconnected—allowing my first angry reactions to pass. I asked for guidance. I prayed to my "higher-ups" to be allowed to hear Maximo. (Regarding those "higher-ups": as I said before, everyone defines and perceives spirituality and spiritual guidance in unique ways. When I was four or five years old, I stuck a bobby pin into a wall socket. The shock threw me across the room, but somehow—miraculously—it didn't kill me. I heard a clear voice say, "You're lucky I was here. That could have stopped your heart and taken your life." I stored that little incident away. Later, meditations revealed that I had a number of spirits helping me, spirits who were always with me—comprising what I've come to think of as a bouquet of incredible masters, all of whom I now call on for guidance.)

Helped by my meditation and prayers, I realized in that moment that screaming at Maximo would simply have been replaying my own history, when my mother screamed at me and made me stay in my room until my father could get home to punish me. When you're repeating your history, you've lost yourself. You fall into an anger that you unfairly pass on to your child. When I finally sat down with Maximo and asked him what was bothering him, at first he couldn't tell me. Then he said, "You've been on the phone for 101 hours!" In fact, I *had* had a busy morning on the phone. I told him that I sometimes had to talk to people on the phone, but that didn't mean I didn't care about him. Then Maximo finally said, "I feel really sad right now." His voice was so soft and quiet that he touched my heart, and I hugged him. He had finally expressed what he was really feeling; he had finally felt safe enough to tell me. And while this didn't instantly make him happy, it did relieve a lot of his tension. He calmed down. He was able to be a little more patient. But most important, he'd received the time and attention he was trying to tell me he really needed. Rather than ending up in an angry screaming match, we ended up hugging each other.

Whenever you're around your children, you're communicating with them, through words or body language, directly or indirectly; they're aware of every move you make. You're their number-one role model. What you say and do is what they'll believe should be said and done until they're old enough to analyze their past (and, if necessary, heal themselves). Sometimes you need to apologize to your child. Once, when Maximo was hoarding his toys and acting mean toward Zoë, I heard myself say to him, "Cut it out. You're not being nice. You're mean." Maximo's eyes grew wide. He thought I was telling him—and I was, of course, though I didn't mean to—that *he* was mean, not just his behavior. I instantly apologized: "I'm sorry I said that you're mean. You aren't mean; you're *acting* mean. You're a wonderful boy and I love you. But right now you aren't acting like it." Even though Maximo was only five years old, he understood. And sometimes he apologizes to me too. He says something that's become a family phrase: "Do you apologize my acceptance?"—mixing up the words a little, but getting the point across.

The point here is that your own behavior is your most effective teaching tool. If you don't help your neighbor, your children won't help their neighbors. If you curse, they'll curse. If you speak ill of others, they'll speak ill of others. Most everything we parents do, our children will consciously or unconsciously repeat. If what they see in us is negative or destructive, they'll spend years feeling off-balance, living dysfunctionally. All we have to do to prevent this is take full responsibility for our words and behavior and be clear about what we're communicating to the precious souls in our care.

A large part of communication involves listening. Communication can be deadly if one party tries to explain something to another without respecting the boundaries or perspective of the person who's receiving the explanation. To avoid chaos and turmoil in communication, we must remember never to communicate with malice or negative intent. When faced with an uncomfortable situation, communicate from the heart, not from fear. When your child says something that upsets you, don't attack him. Try saying, "I don't understand where you're coming from right now." This is an invitation to your child to tell you what he's really feeling. If I had simply yelled at Maximo on his whiny day, I would never have received the gift of important information that he finally gave me: telling me he was feeling sad.

When you want to communicate something to your children, ask them to listen with an open mind and let them know you want to hear how they feel after you're done. The fear of open and honest communication is often worse than the reality of allowing the words to come out of your mouth. Children are born without this fear of communication, intimacy, and love. It's only through negative experience that they close themselves off. Let them express themselves, and express yourself to them, and you'll be creating the positive experiences children need to keep their hearts open and their minds growing.

What about children communicating with each other? Often problems stem from one child's not wanting to share something—usually a beloved toy—with another child. Sharing is always an issue with children. It isn't necessarily that children don't want to share; sometimes they're *afraid* to share. They may not know what sharing really means. A child may fear that if she gives up a favorite toy to a playmate, she'll never get it back. Maximo has a musical toy that Zoë wanted to play with. Whenever she grabbed for it, Maximo would freak out. I explained that letting Zoë play with the toy didn't mean he'd have to *give* it to her; he'd get it back. But this didn't hold water with Maximo. His fear of losing the toy was too strong. Then I wondered: What was it about this toy that made him feel so possessive? Later he told me he was afraid Zoë might break it. He didn't think she'd take as good care of it as he did. Rather than lecturing him on how important it is to share, I suggested that he keep it out of sight when Zoë came over and let her play with toys he didn't feel so strongly about.

Sharing is something children learn about slowly. It may be easier at first to teach them to share with objects in which they don't have a huge investment. It's important to respect a child's fear of giving something up that he or she loves. Once again, the best way to teach children to share is to demonstrate sharing in your own behavior. Let your children see you freely give to others, and they'll learn to give freely too.

Express appreciation to your children when they tell or show you the smallest detail of life. Let them know you're listening, and affirm that you'll *always* listen. When Maximo was about two and a half, Michael and I hosted a big holiday party. As I worked in the kitchen, readying coffee and cake for the fifteen people waiting in the living room, Maximo took two big spoons out of the kitchen drawer. He held them up to me with a questioning look, so I told him what I use them for. He had another vision, however; he saw them as tools for cleaning the kitchen floor. As I made the coffee, he pretended to clean the entire floor, digging the spoons into corners, banging them on the kitchen tiles. A lot of work for one child. After he was done, he made it very clear that he had cleaned a lot. He needed to hear my approval and praise. It took all of five seconds to give it to him.

Maximo was convinced that he was helping me with his spoons, which brings up an important point. Our children have a right to their opinions, whether or not we, in our own childhood, were taught otherwise. Please don't ever stop your children from expressing their thoughts. Encourage them to be open. If what comes out of their mouths is hurtful or mean or negative, you may need to explain what they just said and how it sounded to you. Then help your children to process the feelings of sadness, loneliness, or anger that underlay their "mean" words. If they can't get to their feelings, call a time-out: tell your children that you don't need to talk about it just then, but don't forget to bring it up later. Remember: these childhood years go by fast, and you're building a foundation that your children will have for a lifetime. It's truly up to you to help your children build a strong, loving, healthy life. Understanding, love, and patience are the keys to fulfilling this responsibility. Your reward is a most unbelievable closeness and love.

Communication like this applies to us all, young and old. We're never too old to start communicating. Get a handle on the need for back-and-forth conversation.

Allow yourself to be open enough to receive what's being said to you; then respond with your true feelings. Don't stop the conversation because you don't like what you hear. If you're puzzled, always let the speaker know it's not clear to you what she's trying to say. If the speaker happens to be your child, and you don't like what you hear, stop. Take the time to figure out where he's coming from. You've made the commitment to listen, and if you don't live up to that commitment, you have to be prepared for the consequences: a child who will have a hard time feeling safe communicating with you.

As your child is growing, keep talking and keep listening. Children always let you know when they're ready to process the information you give them. Don't predetermine your child's ability to grasp a thought or idea. If you don't try to explain what's on your mind, you'll never know. One of my favorite stories stars my own son. Maximo was three years old and understood the meaning of Christmas. He understood the celebration of the birth of Jesus. He understood the beauty of the lights and the decorations. He loved and understood the presents under the tree, knew that Santa was Father Christmas and the reindeer carried Santa everywhere. He felt the joy and love of being with family and friends, and of sharing. He really understood the cookies and the cakes and the candles. And he loved it so! But then came Easter, and we started to celebrate again with decorations, pretty spring colors, painted eggs, and of course the Easter Bunny. When he wondered when we'd be putting the tree and the outside lights up and asked about presents for this festive occasion, I tried to explain Easter to him. My three-year-old son, with all his glorious ability, couldn't understand what I was saying. When he asked if the Easter Bunny was with Jesus at the manger, I realized he just wasn't ready to process the information, no matter how I explained it. I stopped trying to overload his circuits with explanations, waiting instead until he was ready. Children let you know when they're ready to receive the information you have to offer them.

Always give your children—or anyone, for that matter—the benefit of the doubt. If someone is acting strange in a situation, most likely he or she is afraid or uncomfortable in the moment. Go somewhere safe, away from the tense circumstance you're both facing. Talk about your feelings without demanding understanding of them. If your son doesn't understand his feelings, offer to help to sort them out by listening and creating a safe place to explore them. If he's really holding back, however—apparently just plain afraid to communicate—you may need to seek outside help. It may be that he's afraid of being punished and needs a reassuring third voice.

Punishment should never be the consequence of telling the truth. As a parent/guardian, you need to know why your child behaved in a way that caused you concern. After your daughter explains her actions, tell her why what she did was wrong. If the incident occurs again, repeat the process. You know, from personal experience, that it sometimes takes a few repetitions before you learn your lessons. The same is true for your child. Patience, understanding, and honesty make far better tools for learning than punishment, especially when it's rendered without explanation.

What about the often-repeated rule about father and mother presenting a united front? Rarely true. I strongly believe parents shouldn't hide their arguments. For one thing, children always sense tension between their parents and may privately come up with horrifying scenarios about what's going on—often blaming themselves. Don't hide your disagreements. The best medicine is to show your children how you work through difficulty; then your children can learn that it's possible for two people to work things out. Allow your children to have separate relationships with each of their parents:

they'll more than likely react differently to Mommy than to Daddy. This is normal and good. We each have separate bonds to each other that need to be cherished, not criticized.

One of your children may turn out to be an effective negotiator or peace-keeper. Michael and I have always had a war over the phone bill: he's usually convinced it's astronomical, because he's not a phone person and thus rarely makes calls. I, on the other hand, *am* a phone person, and I'm willing to pay the price for that. Recently, when we'd gotten into our old tug-of-war on the subject, Maximo piped up, "All right! Enough already. You've both said the same thing a hundred times." Michael and I stopped, surprised. "You're right," we said. Maximo's comment gave us a needed break. Michael asked me, "Could you at least try to make long-distance calls when the rates are cheaper?" I agreed. Maximo wasn't afraid to get involved, because he knew that Michael and I weren't involved in anything dangerous. We had shown him, over and over, that everybody disagrees and that the world doesn't come to an end when you don't see eye to eye. Max even felt free enough to help us come to a solution!

Sometimes you ease your way to communicating by pausing a moment, reflecting, and allowing yourself to meditate—or pray. Prayer can be a very important preparation for interpersonal communication. It's communication with your higher power, and we need to take the same approach with prayer as with people. Openness and honesty, free and without fear: this is what we need to practice. I've told you about my own bouquet of spirits: they bring me so much peace and clarity. Explore your own connection to prayer. And suggest to your children various ways to meditate, to look within. It may be part of your religion; it may be something that arises out of your own private experience. In either case, talk about it with your children, and teach them to respect the wondrous variety of religious and prayer rituals that exist on this planet. Let your children experiment with different forms of prayer and discover what works for them. Prayer isn't only about communicating with God; it's also about communicating with yourself, being honest to yourself about your feelings, hopes, and fears. If your children can learn to be open and honest with themselves, they'll be open and honest with everyone they communicate with as they take their journeys.

Our journeys through life require us to communicate with others. There are no rules. Only fear and insecurity prevent us from opening up to the love and power that are all around us. Remember that the root of anger is fear. If a child displays anger, she's in fear. Search out what that fear is rather than punishing her for her anger. Children aren't born with fear and insecurity. And remember that our children emulate us. If we show consideration, compassion, and love, then that's what we'll fill their hearts and lives with forever.

SIX

❧ *The Grace of Discipline*

When most of us hear the word *discipline*, something inside us usually clenches. We remember the harsh words and punishments doled out to us by our own parents or teachers. We remember other people's attempts to control us. As parents, we may also think of, and perhaps feel a bit uncomfortable about, our attempts to discipline our own children—to exercise control over their behavior, often in ways that mirror the ways by which we ourselves were controlled. In no other area do we more often do what was done to us—even though, consciously, we may have made a pact with ourselves: "I won't be like Mom and Dad in that way." But when anger and frustration mount, our first impulse is often to do exactly what our parents did to us.

If we experienced verbal disrespect and or physical violence in our upbringing, we need to break this cycle of abuse, hard as it often is to do so. It is time to change our views of discipline, to embrace the positive, loving aspects of this art. Yes, discipline is an art, but only when it's motivated by love and done for the sake of the soul—both the child's soul and your own. The aim of discipline isn't to apply constraints to another human being; it's to cultivate a sense of responsibility in someone else—to help that person to develop his or her sense of *self*-discipline. This also describes the aim of this chapter: to help you to embrace discipline as a loving art and to get away from the dictatorial position we normally think of when we hear the word *discipline.*

When respect and love motivate you, discipline doesn't mean imposing your will on your child, directing his or her behavior so that it conforms to your idea of how your child should behave. It becomes a way to open up a dialogue between you and your child, inviting both of you to come to a shared solution between equal souls about how to live with each other in the most productive possible way. This emphasis on a shared solution produces what I think of as a state of "grace": a context of love and respect in which both you and your child define and honor each other's limits, coming to compromises that meet the needs and wishes of both of you as much as possible. Discipline is always a team effort. Working with your child (or children) as a team will spontaneously produce that state of grace that is the goal of discipline: balance, forgiveness, and a willingness to work together toward a common goal.

Something that happened recently with Maximo and Zoë illustrates what I mean. We were playing in the pool, splashing each other, racing, getting rambunctious. As Max and Zoë got more and more riled up, their play began to go over the edge; the pushing got a little too rough, the splashing a bit out of hand. I knew we needed to wind down, and my first impulse was to say something like, "Okay, that's it. Calm down!" But I knew I couldn't just *say* it; they were too wild for that. I had to find some way to help them wind down. I also knew that, to be effective, it had to be a team effort. They had to *want* to wind down on their own if we were going to accomplish this without anger and tears.

I needed to change their vision. "Okay, now listen to this," I urged. Squinting at the distance and pointing, I said, "I see a castle over there." Max and Zoë suddenly stopped. "Where?" they both asked me. "Don't you see? Over there!" I pointed again. The children jumped into this game of pretend eagerly. "How many windows do you see in the castle?" I asked them. Maximo said, "Sixty!" Zoë joined in: "I see a queen. She has sapphire earrings and a beautiful necklace." Max said, "I see horses outside the moat around the castle." Zoë added further embellishment: "The queen is waving to the horses!" As Max and Zoë came up with more and more details, they slowly calmed down; their energy was shifting from outer to inner. By the time they'd finished visualizing the castle, they'd calmed down on their own. I'd managed to find a way we could *all* wind down—not by imposing "the law," but by beckoning them to shift gears on their own. "Discipline" worked because it was a team effort. We *all* joined into the process; as a result, by degrees, we all were able to wind down.

Each of us is an individual, and we each need our own individual boundaries. But the difference between positive boundaries and freedom, or negative boundaries and forced control, lies in the outcome. When discipline is used negatively, it begins to create dysfunction; when we feel forcibly controlled, when we feel that our freedom is being denied, we experience anger and a diminished sense of self-worth. Smothering your child's spirit with negative boundaries prevents him or her from taking chances and positive risks due to the fear of change, keeping him or her from pursuing adventure in life. In past generations rather universally (and in the present generation all too often), discipline was so intertwined with forced respect and control that it produced fear. But respect gained through fear isn't true respect; true respect can be earned only through positive discipline—discipline motivated by love. Positive discipline, applied with loving intentions, helps create a balanced, well-intentioned individual who feels understood, not slapped down or controlled.

But I know from painful experience how hard it is sometimes to make discipline positive. When Maximo was about three, he had already picked up quite a few four-letter words. He couldn't help hearing them in the world around him, and he soaked them up like a sponge. He saw how they shocked people, and sometimes— gleefully—he'd use one or two of them to shock me. I'd explain that they weren't nice words and weren't acceptable in public—that I might slip sometimes and use one or another of them, but it wasn't acceptable from me either, and I apologized whenever I did. But he loved the sound of these words. He'd slip one or two in whenever he could—and I must say he used them quite appropriately in context. I tried many different approaches: the stern "No, we don't talk like that" command, the don't-pay-attention-to-it ploy, and the "Remember what I said about using that language!" approach. Then came a day when he was playing with the four-year-old son of a guest. That boy was tearing through Maximo's toys with no respect. My son got so upset that he told the boy's mother, who took her son aside for a moment, but still the friend didn't stop. Soon I heard Max come tearing down the steps in a frustrated rage. Facing the boy's mother he thumped his fist on his chest, then opened his arms wide and announced, "I'm a Power Ranger, and he's a fucking asshole!" I was aghast. I excused us and took him into another room to explain that what he'd just done wasn't acceptable. I told him that the next time he talked that way there'd be a time-out—and if that didn't work, he wouldn't get any small toys or gifts for a long time. (There's nothing wrong with rewarding your child for behaving respectfully and with compassion. Your gifts don't have to be expensive or store-bought; they can be something you or your partner has that your child would love to own, such as a screwdriver or a necklace or a pencil kit. When you share in this way with your children, you're saying that you're proud of the loving way they're growing up.)

There were many apologies from Max that day, but that little soul has a very strong will. One day not long after this episode, we were at a bake sale helping his school to raise some money. He came outside and asked me at lunch for his umpteenth piece of chocolate something. I explained to him that he couldn't have any more. Pumped with sugar, he turned to me—in front of his classmates and some other mothers—and said, "I don't give a fuck. I want more." Well, it was time for us to go home. I was so angry that what I *feared* would happen, happened. He had once again used foul language inappropriately in public. I reacted with negative discipline. We both got into the car and I closed the windows so I could holler at him all the way home, telling him he'd overstepped his boundaries by using language I'd asked him to stop using. I yelled and threatened: "You won't have this" and "You won't have that." I was out of control. Maximo was not used to my acting this way. I upset him so much. He didn't act like himself for the rest of the day. He was nervous, uncertain of my every move, and fearful. I'd pushed with negative discipline, frustrating him so severely that he wasn't able to communicate his feelings.

So I pulled myself together aand pologized for my reaction—I was angry and out of control. I sat down with him once more to explain what we'd need to do if he continued using this language. But now I allowed him his own little discipline. I told him that if he could keep that language to himself in his bedroom, he was allowed to say and think the words. He couldn't use them outside his room, however, and never with anyone else in his room. That became his discipline, and we never had a problem again after that. He came to me and reported when he heard questionable language—"I heard a bad word again, Mommy!"—letting me know that he knew that bad words were inappropriate to say in public.

Positive discipline works because its aim isn't to kill the child's spirit; on the contrary, its aim is to give the child guidelines he or she can understand and can live within. When you give your child some say, or some room to move, in the management of his or her behavior, you give your child power. Furthermore, your child then doesn't feel as if his or her thoughts and feelings are wrong. With positive discipline, you allow your child to understand that some *behaviors* are unacceptable but that a person's *feelings* are always acceptable. When discipline is a team effort, you can help your child to put a rein on acting on those feelings in certain inappropriate ways while giving space for your child to express those feelings. You don't kill the spirit; you give it a "pot" to grow in.

If many of us, as children, had undergone Maximo's bake sale experience, we would have been slapped, or had our mouths washed out with soap, or been told go to our room (and not come out). This is what I experienced, certainly, and it's a wonder it didn't entirely break my spirit. I know from my own experience of negative discipline that when it's used, it builds up a wall of fear, distrust, and anger that rarely gets broken down when you move into adulthood. Even in children who are loved by their parents, the experience of negative discipline badly shakes any safe bond they may once have felt with those caregivers. Luckily, as happened with me in dealing with Maximo after the bake sale, even when you give in to the first impulse to punish negatively, you can quickly redirect the boat.

Recently a divorced friend of mine, the father of a three-year-old girl, was over visiting with his child. He mentioned that his daughter had been a "bad girl" the previous night at dinner. Normally I don't interfere with other people's parenting, but I couldn't hold myself back when I saw how hurt and uncomprehending the little girl looked at her father's announcement. I said to her, "I know you're not a bad little girl. Something you did may have been bad, but you're not a bad girl." The father said, "But you don't understand. She was a monster at the dinner table last night—throwing food, dropping her fork and spoon on the floor, scream-ing." He explained that she'd settled down only when he'd threatened to buy a cat, a creature that the little girl was terrified of. She was then too petrified to move. I turned to her father and said, "Don't you realize you're this child's king? Why would you make her fear her king? She was probably tired and needed comfort, not fear." The father, teary-eyed, said he now understood the full force of the damage he'd done to his little girl. He was upset because he could remember that same damage being done to him. He then told his daughter she was never ever a bad girl; she just sometimes did bad things. He assured her that she should always be-lieve she was good.

So many other stories of negative discipline crowd my mind—as I'm sure they do the memories of your own childhood, and perhaps (even more painfully) the memories of how you've treated your own children. I was once in an ice-cream parlor in New Jersey, standing in line with my son. My gaze fell on a family with a little girl who was looking around the parlor with amaze-ment, just observing. But she was staring at people, and her father didn't like it. He slapped her arm and said with great force, "Turn around! Don't look at anyone!" I'll always remember the look of shock on her face. The slap was a punishment entirely uncalled-for, coming from someone with whom she ought to have felt safe. In the colorful environment of the ice-cream parlor, it was completely natural that she would want to look around and investigate, to get comfortable with strange surroundings. Her father overstepped her boundaries and her needs with negative discipline—and all because he felt it was inappropriate for her to look at other people. That's smothering! I'm sure his negative discipline caused a great frustration in her—the kind of frustration that builds through a lifetime, growing with each new act of negative discipline. All he had to do was ask her politely to sit in her chair and turn around, explaining that it's okay to look but not to stare. But he didn't allow her even to look; he was stifling her curiosity and her watchfulness, not allowing her the freedom to observe and learn.

Raising a child in fear is unnecessary and cruel. Respect isn't a function of fear. Fear is used to control in the place of true, loving discipline. It creates frustration and noncommunication, and parents and children can lose each other in the negativity. Children who are afraid of a parent will be afraid of life, afraid to experience, afraid to take risks. They'll hear in their heads that loud, negative *no* that they heard so often—and very probably learn that yelling is the only way to express anger and/or assert oneself.

The word *no* is powerful. Use it wisely, and only when necessary. And when it *is* used, it needs to be followed by a patient explanation. Sound itself is also powerful. Raise your voice sternly only in extreme circumstances, when there's possible danger. If you constantly yell at your children, they'll become so desensitized to the sound that they may not respond quickly enough in a life-or-death situation.

Respecting boundaries is the key to positive discipline. It's fine to create certain boundaries for your children, but they must be flexible enough to accommodate the individual soul's journey. Remember that children have boundaries too—boundaries that they themselves have established—and you must respect those if they're healthy. This can be hard to remember, especially when your child does something that pushes your buttons—makes you very angry before you've had a chance to step back, take a deep breath, and try to see the larger picture. One morning a while back Maximo was getting a little too physical with Zoë—roughly shoving her when he walked by her, pushing her out of the way. Not that Zoë was a saint in the scenario: she had in fact provoked him. She was playing the older sister, teasing and baiting him, annoying him with taunts. But then, after the third or fourth time Maximo had pushed her really hard, she flinched when he walked by—expecting to be hit or shoved again. I hated to see her react with so much fear (it reminded me of how I used to react to my own abusive father), and I got angry: "You don't want people to react fearfully to you, Max! Go to your room and think about that!" My words weren't inappropriate, but my tone was. Because I was yelling at Maximo, all he really heard was that I'd raised my voice. Without meaning to, I'd been as verbally violent with him as he'd been physically violent with Zoë. I'd stepped over *his* boundaries. Maximo did go to his room, but I walked in after him and apologized for losing my temper. I explained calmly and simply why he had upset me. He said, "But Zoë was *bothering* me!" I acknowledged that Zoë could sometimes be a pain but added that there was rarely an excuse to react by shoving or using any physical force. It was a great time to explain self-defense, which I said should never be physical unless you're actually threatened with physical danger and need to protect yourself. Now, because I was calmer and listening to Maximo, he could hear and understand my words, not simply react to an angry tone. Our boundaries were restored—which also meant respect and love and understanding were restored.

Remember that an angry raised voice communicates its own message, one that might be very different from the actual words. When we're screaming, the person we're "communicating" with usually just shuts down or simply yells back at us. At those times, we're not connecting; we're just attacking or defending. Teach your children about respecting boundaries, and the consequences of crossing them—but don't cross their boundaries by yelling at them while saying how important it is to respect boundaries! If you violate this dictum, you're giving a mixed, contradictory message—with the negative half almost always louder than the positive. Help your children to understand boundaries with clear explanations, but also by setting your own example of respecting boundaries yourself. Allow your children to question those boundaries, and let them create their own boundaries, such as times when they want to be alone in their room or with a friend. However, stay alert by gracefully keeping one eye on what's going on—for example, by tapping on the door softly every so often to check in with them.

It always helps to remember how large a part fatigue can play in making us less than patient. Take the time of day into account. By four or five o'clock in the afternoon, you're almost always dealing with a very tired child—and you may be exhausted yourself. Be patient: we tend to say and do things when we're exhausted that we'd never do otherwise. Once, late in the day, Maximo had ketchup on his hand and wiped it on our white couch. I told him at least six times to go into the kitchen and bring out a wet cloth to clean it with, but he ignored me. I then said I thought he needed to spend some time in his room, and I asked him please to do so. I also asked him if he understood why he needed to be disciplined in this way. He looked at me sleepily and said yes, he did understand. He said he was sorry about the mess he'd caused. "But I'm tired, Mommy. Can I go lie down and watch a video? I won't make any more messes, I promise." I looked at him and saw a very tired little five-year-old. I knew it was time to let go—and not hold a grudge about the ketchup. Sometimes discipline has to be delicate: you need to express an abundance of love and lighten up, especially with a one-, two-, three-, four-, or five-year-old child. Be flexible, be understand-ing, say please and thank you, and honor your children for saying please and thank you to you.

If you raise your children with love, using positive discipline, teaching them about boundaries and respect, letting them explore their individual journeys in safety, you'll be granting them the gift of freedom. As a result, they'll take risks carefully, make the choices that help themselves and others, be powerful in their hearts, and respect out of love, not fear—safely going forward in life. You'll be at peace with most of their decisions and trust that they'll find the adventure life holds for them without putting themselves in undue danger.

SEVEN

৶ *Single-Parenting*

When you dedicate time to your children in a two-parent home, where both parents take responsibility, one or the other parent can sometimes relieve the other, give the other time to fulfill individual needs and go back into the grand arena of life. But when you're the only parent, time and dedication are constant, and you may feel as if you'll never get off the merry-go-round. Patience, as always, will turn out to be a large part of your remedy.

While raising God's miracle as a single parent means traveling a road paved with both great joy and great difficulty, it doesn't have to be the nightmare some people make it out to be. What it can be is a dream come true. As a single parent, you're forced to take a good look inside yourself and draw on the positive energy that comes from the love in your heart for your child.

Single-parenting is often a spiritual choice—a partnership chosen by both your soul and your child's soul. A new soul chooses a special single parent for specific lessons in its journey just as you've chosen to be a single parent for the specific lessons in yours. You need to keep that element of choice clear. If you fail to—if you abandon responsibility for a choice both you and your child made—you run the risk of misdirecting your frustration and anger over the difficulties of single-parenting toward your child and the act of childrearing. Frustration, fear, and anger are realities of single-parenting (as they are in any family configuration). In the single-parent home, these emotions may be created by the absence of one partner due to divorce, by one partner's denial of the responsibilities of parenting although both parents still live under the same roof (a partner who's "absent" even though physically there), or by the death of one parent. These painful emotions can be dealt with productively only if you remember that you're in your particular difficult situation not because of your spouse or your child or the unpredictable change of fortune of life; you're there because that's where you can learn the lessons your journey requires.

When you're a single parent, the focus is even more clearly broadened from yourself to include another soul. Zoë's mother, Marilyn, who made the deliberate decision to become a single mother, is especially aware of this shift now that she has a little daughter. She told me that she had lived with such total self-focus before parenthood that her life then, in retrospect, seems shallow and unstructured: she dated different men, partied a lot of the time, lived to gratify her passing desires. But this type of life became gradually less and less satisfying. Her decision to have a child was a decision to feel and share love that hadn't happened for her with anyone else. Love, as Marilyn discovered, also creates structure and a wonderful balance. For the first time in her life, she was able to become spiritually fulfilled. The structure that Zoë's presence has given her life doesn't mean she no longer has fun. But now her spontaneous and instinctual temperament helps her to enjoy sharing life with Zoë. She used to live rather out of focus; now she concentrates on being with the great new spirit she has called forth into the world—her daughter.

Being a single parent is really the same thing as being two parents in one respect: it requires making a huge commitment *all* the time. But the rewards are ongoing as well. For example, having a child led Marilyn to her first real self-healing; she feels her child has taught her far more spiritual lessons than she ever could have imagined were possible. However, as beautiful and all-consuming as this overwhelming love is, Marilyn—along with many other single parents—has discovered that the pendulum can swing too far in the direction of overprotection, overstimulation, and a love that smothers and spoils rather than nurtures and leads to freedom.

This is a common challenge faced by single parents, who sometimes tend to concentrate too strongly on every breath their children take. My cousin once told me a story about his fiancée, who had single-parented her two children for most of their young lives. He loved her devotedly, respected her tremendously, in fact saw her as his soul mate—and thought she was a good mother. However, when they all moved in together, he discovered how little the children were able to take care of themselves. Their mother, although she loved and wanted the best for them, overprotected and overstimulated them by coming to their aid too often. As a result, they never took out the garbage, they left their clothes on the floor, they didn't clean their rooms—in short, they had no idea how to take care of themselves. Their mother saw that this was happening, but she felt so guilty about the lack of a father figure that she couldn't keep from doing everything for them.

In addition to smothering by overprotection, you can smother your child with too much hugging, kissing, and touching. Such an excess can be confusing for the child—sometimes sending a sexual message that you don't intend. There should be a balance in how we express affection. Children need boundaries and some amount of privacy; they need to feel that their space is their own. A single parent should certainly express abundant love, but he or she should also realize that children need space to stand up and grow up in on their own. For similar reasons, it isn't generally a good idea to encourage children to call a parent by the parent's first name—a practice that's common in single-parent households. "Mom" and "Dad" are wonderful names, because they instantly define the roles children need their parents to fill as loving guardians.

While many more men and women are becoming single parents by choice, sometimes single-parenthood is unlooked-for, as when one parent unexpectedly dies. Becoming a single parent due to the death of your child's other parent is a devastating experience for everyone in the family. Your little soul is receiving saddening energy that he can't process or understand. The loss is more painful than he knows. Unfortunately, especially if his mother or father dies when he's very young, he may remember little of that parent. So you're faced with healing your heart and raising your child alone. We should always keep in mind that in life some journeys are longer than others and that time is God's healer. Once again, if your heart is filled with love and respect, your journey is made easier.

One of the most wonderful things you can do for your child is to keep a passed-away parent alive in her heart by telling stories of that parent and keeping pictures around. The child needs to know that she was part of someone else and was loved dearly by that person. Don't pretend it wasn't a loss. It *was* a loss, a devastating reality of your journey. This is a time when your journey is filled with pain. It isn't a hill; it's now a mountain. When your child lets you know that she feels bad about not having a second parent, acknowledge her pain but let her know how grateful you both should be to have each other. Allow yourself and everyone around you to feel the loss, and eventually you'll move out of that feeling and begin to focus on the journey of single-parenting.

Remember: if you do the best you can, if you stay in touch with your positive feelings, if you look at your children not as the cause of your pain but as a great miracle that has the power to heal you through love, you will be rewarded for being a great single parent.

If you haven't yet learned patience, let single-parenting become a calling for your own rebirth, an opportunity to repattern and plant new seeds in your own life. Prayer or meditation is especially healing at this time; it can give you the opportunity to connect with the eternal source of love and strength that exists in each of us on a soul level. Talking with friends, with other members of your family, and especially with a therapist experienced in dealing with grief is also a good idea. This passage can be physically exhausting and emotionally painful, but with love, patience, and support, your picture becomes clear. All the pain isn't forgotten, but the clarity gained from looking within, and from seeking help from others, will make you a better, stronger person and parent.

Perhaps the most important thing to remember as a single parent is to not put blame on your children or anyone else for your difficulties. You need to respect that your role as a single parent is one that your soul and your child's soul have chosen as a means to learn certain life lessons. Even when it seems as if you didn't choose to be a single parent—for example, when you lose your partner to death or to a divorce that you opposed—you might want to consider the idea that, on a soul level, you may well have chosen to go this single-parent route. The reasons we make soul choices are always mysterious, and I'm certainly not suggesting that you "wanted" to be alone or to have someone else die. However, you may still have made a pact with the souls of your child and the other parent to work things out in this particular way, in this particular life. Allowing for this spiritual possibility can lead you to a very deep peace. It will also help you to take responsibility for your own life and for the increased commitment you now have to your child or children.

The positiveness you felt when you chose to bring your child into the world must be held within your heart always. Your child should never feel blamed for the work you must do with and for yourself. Children often assume the responsibility for the loss of the other parent anyway. It's well known that when two parents get divorced, each child feels it was something he or she did. I remember so clearly when my own parents told me they were separating: I told them I would be a good girl, hoping that this would keep them from splitting up.

It's so important to let children know it isn't their fault, to reinforce that they had nothing to do with the change in the family.

Parents must be careful how they manifest the reality of the situation. If you find yourself single due to divorce, for example, be very careful that your anger and frustration aren't turned on your children. These little souls don't deserve to be subjected to your anger. They're not the reason for your divorce; you and your partner are (although your children, like you, are seeking the lessons single-parenting can teach). These children should never be used or abused, put in the middle, or asked to choose sides or feel guilty about loving the absent parent. They should never be given a negative response to their desire to spend time with the other parent. They have nothing to do with the pain of your separation. They'll be dealing with their own pain. Your duty as a loving parent is to help them deal with that pain by allowing them their feelings. Let them talk about the family situation as much as they need to. Never accuse them in a negative way of being like the parent who's gone. That would be unkind and unfair and could produce a separation between you that would last forever. If you notice negative traits that your children seem to have picked up from your expartner, calling those traits to their attention in due time may help—but attacking your children with them forces them to build a wall between you. Your misdirected anger could be the beginning of the end of your relationship.

I've heard single parents say they're worried that their children aren't experiencing life with the other parent. Women worry that their children have no father figure; men worry that their children have no maternal influence. These concerns are valid. Each child naturally needs a balance of male and female influences for his or her emotional health. When the parent of the opposite sex isn't present in a child's life, he or she may not learn emotional interaction with the opposite sex early enough. If this parental combination doesn't exist, turn to a friend or relative to provide loving influence. Sometimes, even in a household with both a mother and father, this can be a good idea—to provide certain helpful experiences the current parent(s) may simply not be temperamentally able to provide.

Our family has a friend, Peter, who's a fix-it genius; every time he visits, Maximo is riveted by Peter's ability to take apart and put together anything. He often asks, "When's Peter coming again?" This points out something important: as much as possible, let your children choose the people whom they want in their life. And never simply hand your child completely over to another adult, however close: start their association with small amounts of time spent together. In the beginning, spend time with both of them yourself. Your child will quickly make it clear to you if he wants that friend to return. If he does, rejoice! Your child will let you know the parent substitute he wants in his life. If you know that your child needs this kind of outside adult influence, do some networking—keep your antennae up. It could be a grandparent, an uncle or an aunt, or a close friend from your past: you do need to reach out. Don't be overly suspicious or protective. You need to be careful not to visit your own fears of being abandoned on your child. Certainly don't think you'll lose your child if she bonds to another outside influence. If you love your child and have treated her with care and respect, you'll have planted deep roots: you needn't worry that she'll stop loving you in favor of someone else.

There are wonderful people out there to help and support you. Every day, week, and month can be handled lovingly with the help of friends and loved ones. Don't be afraid to ask for help. For some people asking for help is uncomfortable; for others it isn't. If it is for you, you must move beyond the discomfort. We're all here to help each other. All of us have our guardians and assistants who help us on our journeys. But, as we explored earlier in Chapter 3 (on the subject of arrival), you must protect your children by always being sure that your support system is made up of positive people. No matter how close a family member supposedly is, if that person's influence is overwhelmingly negative, you must limit his or her influence on you and your child. Not doing so can create chaos in both of your lives and throw you and your children right off your journeys.

Even when you make sure that the influences around you and your child are positive, the demands of day-to-day life as a single parent can sometimes be so consuming that you lose a sense of the larger picture, not permitting yourself to enjoy all the stages of life your little one is living through. Our stages of life, as children and adults, bring us to greater understanding and create different needs. We must understand and re-spect our children's needs throughout all of these stages. Embrace the time you have with your children, the power of living in the moment, for these stages of their lives pass so quickly. You'll be shocked one day to notice that all the time you need just for yourself has actually become yours. And when it does, it may not seem such a prize after all—especially if you feel that you *didn't* embrace the time you might have had with your children as they were growing up.

With or without a partner, it's important to create the balance of love within yourself, for yourself, so you can teach balanced love. What determines this balance? In one sense, love is like a needed nutrient or medication: your children will tell you the dose they need. If Maximo is getting too many kisses, he'll say, "I've had enough." And when he does so, I have to say (at least to myself), "Okay, I get it!" I have to understand that Maximo isn't saying he no longer loves me; he's telling me he needs to reinforce his sense of boundaries. But he also tells me when he needs attention. Once, while I was working on this book and Maximo had no one to play with, he told me he was bored. I looked up from my writing and said, "Maximo, please—you need to find something to do on your own. I really have to work on my book." Maximo looked me in the eye and said, "Mom, I've been doing that for weeks now." He stopped me dead in my tracks, because he was right. He'd been very good about leaving me alone to work when I needed time to myself, and of course he hadn't been left alone for weeks—but to him it felt like it. So I put down my pen, hugged him, and told him he was right—and we went for a bike ride for an hour or so. When you've unwittingly ignored your children's needs and/or over-disciplined them, the distress on their faces will tell you if you've overstepped their bounds. Let your children tell you what they need—when to feed them, when to stop feeding them. That's how to find the balance of love.

In the case of single-parenting, teaching children about what they do have instead of what they don't have helps them not to live in worry and concern about their lives. Living in constant worry can paralyze a person, letting him or her live life without experiencing it. The parent who passes this kind of fear on to a child paralyzes that child's ability to continue on his or her journey. Instead, teach your child that concern is necessary only when a decision has to be made.

When a little soul enters into life as part of a single-parent situation, single-parenting becomes part of both your journeys. It can be painfully difficult, but love is the best medicine. If you give pure love and respect, and allow each other pure communication, each day will be a grand experience. Through clear understanding, love, and respect, you'll find it easier to go on your journeys and to experience the joy of love between parent and child.

EIGHT

❧ *The Joy of Play*

Play is vital to our lives. Play keeps us happy and healthy and allows us to remove ourselves from the overserious-ness that life often imposes. But play has been misused and misunderstood for generations. As caretakers, we need to understand the balance of play in life so that we can pass that gift on to the children of the world. We need to teach the purity and sincerity of play and guide our children to that blissful place of freedom.

What we need to do is to awaken—possibly re-awaken—our *own* desire for and understanding of play so that we can see and feel how important this aspect of life is. Too often we limit the joy and the balance of play in our children because our own parents limited joy and balance for us when we were children. This chapter will help you to embrace the joy of play, help you to recognize the negative patterns you may need to break so that you can discover how wonderful play can really be—not only for your children but for you.

Instinctively, as small children, we longed to play. When we were infants, we wanted—without fear—to touch, communicate with, and play with anyone who came our way. When we were toddlers, we started to develop our personalities, and it's at this stage that programming patterns were established by parents regarding many issues—one important one being play. For some of us, these were positive and balanced. For others, play became a serious problem because of negative patterns being reinforced by parents and caretakers who had no understanding of the importance of play.

I'm not saying all adults were fed negative play patterns in childhood, but in dysfunctional homes play has long been used (unconsciously, for the most part) to manipulate children; in other words, it's been held over their heads as a privilege that they need to earn. When we were children, some of us heard, "If you don't behave, you can't go out to play," or "If you don't finish everything on your plate, you can't play with your friends after dinner." Play is still often used by parents to bribe and manipulate children, especially very early in life. When those children become adults, play can cause a knee-jerk guilt feeling. Yet if guilt is the emotion that accompanies play, how can we ever play completely, in the fullest, freest sense of the word?

As I grew to understand the necessity of play in my life, I realized that there were many people who shared the misfortune of not understanding the importance of play. Play for me as a child wasn't always safe or comfortable. My mother never took the time to play with me (she was always ill), and my dad rarely did. When I was about five or six, my father taught me how to ride a bicycle. He ran next to me while I wobbled down the street, holding me up. I felt so proud that my dad was playing with me, teaching me to ride a grown-up bike, paying attention to me. But that was one of few times I can remember his giving positive, playful attention to me. That pride turned into hurt and frustrated anger, especially when he referred (again and again) to this one of few moments of shared time as proof that he did play with me. Sadly, my parents didn't understand the need they themselves had for play, so of course they didn't understand their children's need for it. All they knew about playtime was that it could be a reward they could withhold to control their children.

"You can't go out to play," they might say. "Your room is too messy." It would have been more positive for me to hear, and for my parents to have said, "You should have your playtime, so could you please first straighten your room before you go out to be with your friends?"—with compliance accompanied by a thank-you. If you take this sort of stance with your children, you let them know that play is as essential to them as any other aspect of life and that you want them to enjoy their playtime, not earn it as if it were a nonessential luxury. If their rooms remain a mess, you might sit down with them and explain that taking responsibility for cleaning up will give them more time for play—with the message that you *want* them to play, that play is as important as making their beds or putting away their clothes. It's possible that you may hear back from them, "It's not as fun to clean up as it is to play." That's certainly true, and they deserve the confirmation that you know how they feel. Let them know, too, that you're pleased that they understand the importance of taking care of their rooms (or of whatever else you need them to do, or they need to do for themselves) before playtime. Once again, what you're after is *balance:* not the message that work is more important than play but the message that both are important—indeed, essential—in their lives.

A failure to learn early in life this balance between work and play can create real problems with social skills, in some cases creating very sad adults who are never comfortable allowing themselves to have a good time. No matter what they're doing, doubt doesn't allow them the carefree innocence of playing. They're embarrassed or fearful of what people will think, and they're uncomfortable in their surroundings. We must be careful not to instill this doubt into our children. Otherwise, as they grow into maturity, they're left with the uncomfortable feeling that they shouldn't be playing; on those rare occasions when they try to play, they're aware that there's something better or more productive they ought to be doing instead. This attitude can break the spirit. Play teaches the child (and thus the adult) so much about enjoying life and letting go. It offers an essential space for the child's spirit to expand and run free.

Adults who suffer from play deprivation tend to be observers more than participants. They're often uptight, physically tense, and awkward in play situations. They can seem humorless, feel guilty, and possess an inability to express themselves creatively. They're also often judgmental of others who play easily, branding them as immature or childish. Unfortunately, people who suffer from play deprivation unconsciously teach the lessons they learned in childhood to their own children. And that's not all: they also deprive themselves of the pleasure they might have today, playing with their children, exploring possibly for the first time in their lives how much fun it is to have fun!

Not long ago I attended a wonderful workshop given by the Caren Foundation in Pennsylvania, set up to examine the impact of our "family of origin"—the effects of parents on children, and children on parents. One very illuminating exercise required each of us to pick other people in the room to "sculpt" themselves into our father, mother, sister, brother, or other significant member of our first family. We asked the various "sculptees" to adopt whatever body language or position we felt was most typical of the family member they were standing in for. I asked one woman to lie down on a bed—the position that my mother most often adopted with me because she was so often ill. Then I asked a man to stand up with his back to me, facing the wall—a posture symbolic of my father. I had another woman stand in front of me with her arms outstretched, vertical palms outward, as if pushing me away; I then had her say, "Stay away from me! I want nothing to do with you!" She represented my sister. We were encouraged to say whatever we wanted to say to these stand-in mothers, fathers, and siblings, working through painful emotions, telling them what we'd felt unable to tell them as children. It was a remarkable and heart-wrenching experience. It connected me with the full force of the pain I'd felt as a little girl—and made it absolutely clear how necessary it was for me to reprogram myself even more than I had already done, to change the negative assumptions and expectations my fearful parents had unconsciously instilled in me. I saw more clearly than ever before the damage that had been done to me, the results of my poor upbringing.

But it was just as instructive to see other people act out their own family scenarios. So many suffered from not being considered an individual, forced to live their lives in total accordance with their family's dysfunction. They were unfocused, unhappy, lost souls, struggling to stand up on their own and proceed with their own journeys, to accomplish what it was they came into this world to accomplish.

Every day at this workshop we had a designated playtime. Some people were eager to play various sports and games, but many never played at all, choosing to sit on the porch and observe everybody else. Among those who did play, there were some who weren't affected by allowing themselves to let loose—play came naturally to them—and there were some who played hard to avoid their lives. Among those who didn't play, or at least couldn't play without a struggle like me, because very early in life they'd had to become responsible for themselves and didn't know how to play—seriousness was the only route. Play was too hard for these people, because their guard would have had to be let down.

The clear message was that for little souls, starting in infancy, play is imperative. An infant needs to hear the sound of your silly joy and laughter. For example, show your baby a black-and-white toy (the only colors a newborn can see); tell him what the toy is, move it, shake it like a rattle, and let your words and expression show your enthusiasm. Lie down on the bed or floor with him: bring yourself physically down to his level. He'll love it. Always search for little games you can play. These are bonding and developmental times for you and your child. Playtime is a big part of development, and it's necessary if you want your infant to be as happy and healthy as possible.

As our infants become toddlers, we should encourage their playtime and offer our own participation; we should run, jump, and play with them. For some of us—

especially those who are young parents—jumping and running is easy, but I found physical exertion to be a particularly difficult part of being an older parent. When I was playing baseball with my toddler and he asked, "Could you get me that ball?" (meaning the eightieth missed ball of the game), I would turn to God to ask for more physical strength: "Oh, please, I'll do anything you want me to. Just don't make me feel this tired!" But I kept playing because I knew how important it was for my son and me to play together.

This brings up another point: repetitive play. Like a golden retriever who can't get enough of throw-the-ball, your baby or toddler will often want to repeat the same play pattern again and again. It might be peeka-boo, a variation on throwing and retrieving a ball (as with my playing baseball with Max), or a game such as tag or hide-and-seek. Whatever the "sport," you may eventually get a feeling not unlike gagging when you've eaten too much: the idea of running around the back-yard one more time seems impossible. "I can't endure one more moment of this!" you think. Well, sometimes you need to push ahead anyway. It won't kill you to do it for five more minutes—especially when it brings such joy to your child. Then you might employ some of the wind-down team-effort tactics I talked about in the chapter on discipline: distracting your child with a story, getting him or her to participate in shifting gears and calming down with you. Give yourself a time limit (such as five more minutes) when you're reaching the end of your rope—then, together with your child, "play" your way to a new and calmer game, something you both can do to break the pattern and get some rest.

Sometimes other playmates can help you out—and they don't even have to be human! One saving grace for play when I was a child, because I had very little play-time with my parents or sister, was my dog. A pet is the most wonderful playmate and source of unconditional love you can have. A dog isn't just "man's best friend"— it's often best playmate, best sit-while-you're-sick-mate, best I-love-you-forever-mate. For children, animals can be vital to life. They teach us how to become gentle and loving. Maximo is growing up with three standard poodles, two lovebirds, and two turtles. In a household with small children, it's parents who take on the com-mitment to care for animals, but the rewarding lessons are extraordinary.

When your child is an adolescent, play can take many forms, most of them involving even more physical exertion than toddlers can tolerate: Little League sports, biking, roller-skating, swimming—the possibilities are endless. We should still spend playtime with our children if they want us to, but we need to make sure their own participation is voluntary. It's important to support our children in sports, but we must never force them to play a sport because we think they should. It's unfair of us to push them, and parental pressure can cause tremendous anxiety. We can introduce a sport or other activity, but we must allow them their choice and support whatever choice they make. They need to know that play is important enough that we can still enjoy playing with them or observing them having a good time. So if you can't roller-blade, take your bike and ride along. Go to their games. It's so important for them to see you in the bleachers or know that you think their play is important enough to take the time to show up. Encourage them to play and to have fun. This would be a good time to teach them that practice makes *better,* because they're already perfect.

Whether we're children or adults, sometimes our dreams of what would be fun are thwarted by our fear of what someone else will think. That fear causes us not to share our ideas for fun. Yet just as we communicate our feelings about other matters on an emotional level, we must communicate our feelings about play, opening up avenues of play for ourselves, family, and friends. Just start a little; it will feel better and better, and soon you'll do it more and more. When I watched Maximo lose himself in silly, goofy play in his early years, my initial reflex was envy: How could he do it? Why couldn't I play so unselfconsciously, so joyously? At these times, Maximo once again became my teacher. I trusted him to teach me about play, and he did. He still does. I love to dance and sing, and we dance and sing a lot—to all kinds of music. It helps me to release my soul—to tolerate and get beyond my own resistance to full, all-out play. Let your child teach you about play. Stop at the park and play on the swings with her, or with your child's playmates or your own friends. Be creative: make up a new ball game; do whatever makes you feel good; let your imagination soar. Maximo and Zoe teach me so much about this: sometimes they play house as husband and wife; sometimes they imagine they're on top of a mountain or lost in a jungle or exploring Mars—whatever scene or game makes them feel good at the moment. That's the essence of what play is: whatever makes you feel good. Step out and do what you want, with yourself and with others. Allow yourself to play, to feel good. You deserve it. Then pass the gift of play on to your children and let them teach you how to play their games. Reach out to play with one another.

Play is supposed to be fun and good and is often ac-companied by laughter, which really *is* the best medicine in life: it feeds the spirit. We must show our new souls that laughter is great! Those of us who live our lives in aware and thoughtful play can teach our children the positive balance of play. Whatever our children's choice of play, it's *their* choice, and we (as loving adults) should always promote and support the action. It's important that we don't live vicariously through our children, pushing them to fulfill some unaccomplished childhood dream of our own. We can present to them the play-ground, we can teach them how to swing, but we can't teach them what to *like* about swinging. Give your chil-dren the ability to create their own play experiences. Look at your own life and examine your own playtime; see if your balance is on or off. If it's off, allow yourself more guilt-free fun time. You'll see a change in your own life. Allowing yourself this freedom will help your chil-dren and your children's children to experience the great joy of playing.

NINE

❧ *Partnership*

Partnership is one of the most powerful phenomena we can embrace. In many ways, this whole book is about the grace of partnership—the ways in which we can learn to work with each other, respecting each other's journeys, and seeking help when we need it. Partnership means learning to listen to what our children, friends, and romantic or marital partners are saying—so that we can help each other's souls to flourish and follow the paths they seek to travel. Perhaps the strongest message I can give you is that you aren't alone. Remember the protection and reassurance I received when I stuck that hairpin into a socket when I was a little girl: I was suddenly made aware that I had angels for partners, looking after me. I've come to think of these spiritual helpers as messengers from God, and I now know they're always with me. They provide a soul partnership that I can always depend on and come back to. God is always with each one of us, however we may perceive God. Whether you're a single parent or with a partner, whether you're contemplating one day having a child or are now in the process of bringing up a whole family of children, remember that you're always in partnership with them as well as with your "higher-ups."

The nine chapters of this book, like the nine months of pregnancy, chart the course we need to take to achieve a spiritual rebirth not only as parents, children, families, and friends but as part of our larger society. Concentrating on partnership draws on all the spiritual lessons we've covered so far in this book. Getting in touch with your inner self, trusting that self and the people who affect you positively, sharing who you are and what you feel and think, taking responsibility, showing respect, and understanding that there's no one right timetable for achieving insight are all key to good partnerships. In this chapter we'll touch on each one of these themes, to help you to understand and achieve the grace and gift of partnership and spiritual rebirth in your own life.

Unfortunately, Western society doesn't help us to understand, cultivate, or enjoy true partnership. Some of the greatest challenges to partnership we face are the negative lessons society has taught us. In the late 1970s and all through the 1980s, much of the world lost the meaning of partnership. Greed set in so powerfully that it was like a plague, and it wiped out the beauty of partnership. *I* and *me* replaced *we* and *us*. Many of our children were taught to "get them before they get you." Many businesses perished; some large industries fell apart; neighborhoods that were once peaceful became unsafe for our children. Our world became unbalanced because selfish greed and distrust spread throughout it, and partnership became a lost theory. We no longer turned to each other for nurturing and support and the strength to carry on through the bad times. Bosses, managers, and business owners lost the sense that employees were as important as they, that without the respected partnership of all workers there could be no strong alliance or thriving business. Neighbors became jealous of each other's material possessions; strong feelings of envy replaced goodwill. People worked at getting bigger and better "stuff" than their neighbors, losing sight of the direction of their own lives. The negative theory of "keeping up with the Joneses" was alive and spreading.

Many children, especially during the past few troubling decades, weren't taught that neighbors are for support and are part of the community, not enemies to mistrust or rivals with whom to compete. When those who are still young grow up, they may never understand the true partnerships they accept when renting an apartment, buying a house, entering a marriage, or bringing souls into the world. They simply haven't been taught that responsibility, caring, sharing, and trust are all essential components of any partnership. So-called yuppies are young people struggling to have it all—or what they think is "all"—but never understanding their loss of partnership and fellowship, losing sight of their individuality and individual journey as they lose themselves in pursuit of somebody else's idea of "the good life," and failing to struggle through the lessons that need to be learned. When we lose sight of our individuality, we can't enter into a partnership.

Michael and I have learned lessons about the role of individuality in partnership in some very personal and sometimes painful ways. It took us a long time before we could appreciate that we were capable of the gift of partnership—that we had in fact made a soul contract to live our lives together. Friends would often tell us that we more than belonged together—that we were really perfect for one another—but it took years of laughter, sadness, turmoil, and even near-separation before we realized this ourselves. The tradition of marriage told us we were uniting as one, but for us marriage seemed to mark the beginning of the end of our partnership. When we got married, we became so "one" that we lost sight of each other's individuality; we tried so hard to be what we thought the other one wanted us to be that we ended up feeling resentful. We didn't realize that true partnership means *embracing* our individuality—not erasing it.

Sometimes when Michael wanted to be affectionate with me, I would get tense and push him away. I couldn't get over the growing resentment over the loss of self I'd felt since the "merger" of our marriage. In great distress I turned to my dear friend Diane Rosenthal, a metaphysician who helped me to feel and welcome a new spiritual presence within me—a gentle female spirit who called herself Arianna. I recognized her as my soft, openhearted feminine side. As I felt her gentle, sweet, loving presence, I began to see Michael differently. He began to emerge for me in a different way. Arianna showed me that it was all right that he and I were different individuals, and that marriage didn't have to mean fighting who he was or who I was. She taught me that through love we could accept and celebrate our unique selves. True partnership means being who you are and living in the moment. As I understood this, my fears lessened, and I allowed love to replace those fears. I not only allowed Michael's love to reach me, but I allowed my own love to come up and touch Michael. I don't know what direction our paths together and as individuals will take in the future. I know only that we need to embrace who each of us is in the moment and experience our partnership in whatever way we need to right now. Partnership now seems freeing to me, not smothering. Michael and I have stopped fighting the soul contract I believe we made to meet and join our paths. We now can experience love for each other and our son as a freedom and a joy.

The most powerful way to become and stay a good partner is first by staying in touch with yourself. We all have a tendency to lose sight of our individuality when we're in a partnership. It's so easy to look at someone else's weaknesses and point them out, but admitting your own is more difficult. Looking at your own weaknesses may cause pain, but that pain is so much less than the pain you create by trying to control or correct someone else's life rather than your own. Trying to control your partner is a road that leads to the end of your partnership. Attempting to impose your will on someone else destroys the balance of true partnership.

In fact, perhaps the most important concept to apply to good partnership is balance: the balance of respecting each other's individuality but realizing that one partner's weakness is another partner's strength. When balance can't be achieved, even through each partner's best efforts, it's sometimes necessary to part ways. Divorce is sometimes essential for two people, in order for them to get back their individuality. In some unhealthy relationships we lose sight of who we are and how great we are and what really good individual gifts we have to offer in our partnerships and in life. We aren't being productive when we don't use our individual strengths to balance our partnerships—or to leave them when we hit an insurmountable block and need, for each partner's well-being, to follow separate paths.

Fortunately, parents don't have to live together to be good partners. Accepting the responsibility of parenthood doesn't require living under the same roof as spouse and children. Not that there aren't painful difficulties when a partnership breaks up. In the wake of a divorce, everyone inevitably suffers: emotions (anger, sorrow, despair) usually run high, and children typically feel they're at least partly to blame for the breakup. It's essential to reassure children throughout this difficult passage that they didn't cause the split between mother and father. If the separation wasn't caused by either parent's abuse of a child, both parents should be equal presences in the child's life. It's terrible that so many judges automatically award custody of children to the mother, exiling the father as if he weren't an equally important presence in the children's lives. Each parent needs to be able to have full and frequent—or "quality"—contact with the children. When my own parents divorced, my father simply stopped being a father; he didn't take responsibility for his parenthood. I used to sit on the stoop waiting for him on the days he was supposed to visit, but he never showed up. Now, as an adult, I realize that my father's need for a mother figure blocked his ability to let a child in: on some unconscious level, *he* had to remain the "child" and therefore wasn't able truly to parent his own children. When he remarried and began a new family, he made no attempt to involve me or my sister in his new life. We were simply abandoned. It taught me a terrible lesson about parenthood, one that it's taken me many painful years to unlearn.

Even if the partnership breaks up, as it does in divorce, you need to respect and adhere to the responsibilities you both still have to the soul or souls you've brought into the world. Make contact in person and by phone: let your children know that you're okay and they're okay and that you can't wait to show them where they'll be in your new life. There's no such thing at this difficult time as too much reassurance. Of course, you need reassurance too; divorce is as difficult for the parents as it is for their children. Seek help from trained professionals or trusted friends. You may receive a good deal of help from your children as well, learning that you can trust in their love for you. It's important to let them know that you don't hate the partner from whom you've divorced. Let your child know that there are different kinds of love: "being in love" is different from the respectful, caring love you'll always try to feel and express for your divorced partner. Don't force your children to take sides. Everybody loses when you turn your partnership into a war.

Trust is the key factor in a true partnership. It's fundamental to your ability to communicate your truest feelings when you need to. If you avoid the openness of trust, you automatically break down the empowered partnership you've set out to create. If a partnership seems not to be working out, there's usually a great lesson to be learned, so it's important not to quit prematurely; instead, plunge deeper into the partnership to get through the lessons you need to learn. That's one of the reasons you're together. Working out life's partnership problems shows your children a healthier way of being a good partner at *anything* in life. You must remember your true intentions when you set out to communicate with your partner.

Partnership involves sharing. I've noticed that good adult partners were generally also good sharers as children. You can't be blatantly selfish and expect to be a good partner or teach the value of partnership. A selfish person always ends up taking the partner for granted, breaking the contract or promise that was made when the partnership was created. This is why we need to teach our children about sharing early in their lives. If you've noticed a problem with sharing in your own life and you know that it's created turmoil in your partnerships, seek help from someone (a therapist, a metaphysician, a clergyperson, or a close friend) who can guide you through this important lesson in your journey.

Remember to be gentle and nonjudgmental about your and your partner's resistances. Just as with siblings, there are no timetables about attaining insights. It takes some of us longer to develop the ability to share than others. Be patient with yourself as well as your partner. Don't take everything your partner says or does too personally. You need to be clear about your own boundaries, but it also helps to understand that you and your partner often act out unconscious scenarios you learned in childhood and that people aren't always in control of their reactions to each other. Sometimes the best thing to do about a storm is let it blow over. But storms that don't pass—impasses that you can't seem to get beyond—may be signs that you need to reach out for help. Remember that if you come to a point in your life when you need to seek professional help, that too is part of your journey. You're opening a door to new ways to think about yourself and your life.

A good partnership happens when each individual is respected for his or her positive aspects and acknowledged—with words—for the part he or she plays in the partnership. "Thank you," "That's great," "What a good idea"—these acknowledgments have tremendous power. Being openly kind and encouraging can do wonders to reinforce the bond between partners. A handshake, a hug, a peck on the cheek, a nod of the head, an okay sign, a high five, and of course a smile—all these are wonderful ways of showing appreciation to your partner or partners.

Respecting your partner's readiness for change or insight is also essential. In this regard, it's important to know that when I speak of partnership, I'm talking not only about the relationship between mother and father. Remember: each parent also has a partnership with his or her children, and children form partnerships on their own, which are just as important. The issue of readiness for change came home to me vividly when Maximo learned to ride a two-wheeler on his own. Some months earlier we had bought Max a bike with training wheels. He said thank you because he knew he was supposed to, but he was wary of this big machine. We told him that the training wheels were there to make him feel comfortable with the bicycle but that eventually they were supposed to come off and he could ride with just two wheels. This concept scared him so deeply that he announced he would wait until he turned five to take the training wheels off. But when he turned five last November, he said he still wasn't ready; he used the bike, but always with the training wheels. In December, when Seth came down for a visit, Max said he was ready to take off the trainers. Seth took the training wheels off and held on to the bike while Maximo got started; then Maximo turned around and yelled, "Seth—let go already!" We all applauded him wildly. When he got off the bike, he came running over to me and shouted, "*Thank you*, Mom—thank you for my bike!" His gratitude was no longer polite: he was thrilled with his bike now that he had become ready to ride it without help. It's clear to me that Maximo's partnership with Seth helped him to reach this breakthrough—and to strengthen his bond not only to Seth but to me as well. Letting in the right person or people at the right time strengthens the partnership network. Our actions always affect and are affected by those of others. We need to explore our potential connection to each other. Be conscious of this connection, and you'll be conscious of the power of partnership.

This consciousness will help you to be sensitive to your child's readiness to connect to other people. You can't push someone to do or say or understand something before he or she is ready. Seth's involvement provides further evidence of this: Maximo responded to Seth because he was *ready* to respond to him. Once you're receptive to being helped, you can have as many partners as you want or need. Don't be afraid to bring in new nurturing presences; always be open to creating new partnerships. When I can't figure out some of lifes problems alone I'll turn to Pamela Cooper or Diane Rosenthal, two very wise and powerful women—Pamela a fairly conventional psychotherapist gifted with great spiritual, loving technique; Diane, as I've noted, a meta-physician (as well as an expert in past-life regression therapy). The context and perspective they give me is invaluable. I regard them as important partners in my life, and I hope to have many more such partners.

I hope the same for my husband and my son as well—and for you too. Reach out for the abundant help that's available to you. Be willing to listen and to speak, to give and to receive. Sometimes you or your partner will become blocked; bring in a third presence to gain perspective—*widen* the partnership to include whatever will help all of you. As I've already suggested, turning to the partnership offered in therapy is often a good idea, especially when you get to a place where you feel you just can't handle things anymore. It isn't productive to blame someone else for your problems—to say, "*He* needs help." *You* need the help to learn how to live with the present struggle.

But always respect the time it takes for you and your partner or partners—spouse, friends, relatives, children—to move to the next stage of the journey. Respecting the fact that we all have different timetables is essential. A passage from Nikos Kazantzakis's *Zorba the Greek* makes this lesson of timing vivid. Zorba speaks of coming upon a cocoon just beginning to break apart to reveal an emerging butterfly. He becomes impatient with the process: he wants to see the finished beautiful butterfly and decides to help nature along by breathing on the cocoon, warming it to speed things up. Kazantzakis writes:

> The case opened, the butterfly started slowly crawling out, and I shall never forget my horror when I saw how its wings were folded back and crumpled; the wretched butterfly tried with its whole trembling body to unfold them. Bending over it, I tried to help it with my breath. In vain.
>
> It needed to be hatched out patiently, and the unfolding of its wings should be a gradual process in the sun. Now it was too late. My breath had forced the butterfly to appear all crumpled, before its time. It struggled desperately and a few seconds later, died in the palm of my hand.
>
> That little body is, I do believe, the greatest weight I have on my conscience. For I realized today that it's a mortal sin to violate the great laws of nature. We shouldn't hurry, we shouldn't be impatient, but we should confidently obey the eternal rhythm.

When we respond to our unclouded instincts, we're responding to our intuition. We know intuitively this truth that Kazantzakis tells us about timing: we know we need to get out of another soul's way so that that soul can find its true path at the pace it alone needs. This intuition is your higher self, your *knower*, helping you to make the right decisions in your own life's journey. So many times when we're faced with decisions, whether about ourselves or the souls in our care, all we need to do is to get *clear*—to separate from the momentary chaos and confusion of daily life and reconnect with our higher self, our intuition. But once we lose contact with this power, once we get out of ourselves and hand over our power to a partner trying to take control, we lose insight, and we teach chaos to our children.

What usually keeps us away from our true selves is one of the most overwhelming emotions in the world: fear. Fear is an emotion produced by the threat of failure or of physical or emotional pain. It's an uneasiness within oneself, a doubting of oneself. If we don't face our fears, we'll fall off our journeys, never having the experience of being good partners, never being in touch with our true selves. Fortunately, the power of love is within all of us—a power that's far stronger than fear. You have the ability to tap into this power any moment you need it. Your soul has many lessons to learn in this life, with the help of others, and it's also chosen other souls in various partnerships to help them learn their lessons. Love—like a butterfly emerging from a cocoon—is the goal all of us seek. Respect the butterfly struggling to be born in you, in your partners, and in the souls of our children.